Mathematics Enrichr

Book C

Anne Joshua

MA, DipEd (Syd), MSc (Oxon)

SIMON & SCHUSTER
EDUCATION

Dedication

To my mother,
my husband Doug
and my children Anthony, Paul and Amanda
for their encouragement and support

Acknowledgment

I thank all my willing guinea pigs, mainly the students of
Moriah College and my daughter Amanda, whose helpful
suggestions were invaluable. I also thank John Smith for
his encouragement.

First published in 1991 by
Longman Cheshire Pty Limited, Australia

This edition published in the United Kingdom in 1993 by
Simon & Schuster Education
Campus 400, Maylands Avenue
Hemel Hempstead, Herts HP2 7EZ

Designed by Norma van Rees
Illustrations by Boris Silvestri
Set in Plantin Light $12\frac{1}{2}/14\frac{1}{2}$ pt.
Printed in Malaysia — TCP

Amendments to the UK edition produced by
Dave Baker and Diana Brightling-Reed

Photocopying
Multiple copies of the pupils' worksheets may be made
without payment or the need to seek specific permission
only by the purchasing schools for use in teaching in
these schools. In all other cases, permission to photocopy
and distribute photocopies of these materials must be sought.

A catalogue record of this book is available from
the British Library

ISBN 0 7501 0566 6

Contents

Attainment Targets

Challenge	Page	1 Using & Applying Maths	2 Number	3 Algebra	4 Shape and Space	5 Handling Data
What's the value?	1	●		●		
Rolling boxes	2	●			●	
Find my rule	3	●	●	●		
Digits and numbers	4	●	●			
Picture graphs	5	●				●
Problem solving: Guess and check	6	●	●			
Problem solving: Working systematically 1	7	●				●
How many?	8	●				
What is my message?	9	●	●	●		
Multiplication table squares	10	●	●	●		
How does it start?	11	●	●	●		
Missing numbers	12	●	●	●		
Number squares 1	13	●	●	●		
Investigating magic squares	14	●	●			
Completing the lines	15	●	●			
Largest and smallest	16	●	●			
Multiplying puzzles	17	●	●			
Counting cubes	18	●	●	●	●	
Halves and quarters	19	●			●	
Puzzles with shapes	20	●			●	
How many routes?	21	●				
Polyiamonds	22	●			●	
Strange maths symbols 1	23	●	●	●		
Letter values	24	●	●			
Problem solving: Working systematically 2	25	●	●			●
Problem solving: Working backwards	26	●	●	●		
Problem solving: Act it out	27	●	●			
Problem solving: Finding several solutions	28	●			●	●
Problem solving: Using tables 1	29	●	●			●
Problem solving: With extra information	30	●				●

Attainment Targets

Introduction

This is the third of a series of four books designed to cater for the mathematically able child.

What is different about this set of books?

These four books have been written to provide a valuable resource of challenging problems for able children of age 7 to 13. The books are much more than a collection of puzzles and difficult problems. The problems are graded and concepts and strategies are developed throughout the series. They provide a systematic development of the pupil's problem solving and mathematical ability. The books may be used to supplement a school's mathematics curriculum and to be integrated into their scheme of work. Each book contains answers, full worked solutions for most problems and valuable suggestions and discussions on many of the problems.

Mathematics Enrichment is a well-structured programme aimed at providing a stimulating environment for able children to learn mathematics. Unless such children are given rich, challenging materials that encourage mathematical thinking they may not fully develop their talents in mathematics. These books provide a source of such material for children between the ages of 7 and 13. The age of pupils using a particular book in the series may vary considerably according to their ability and previous experience. There is a very wide range of mathematical ability between children of the same age and as a rough guide it is suggested that:

    Book A is used by children aged 7 to 10;
    Book B is used by children aged 8 to 11;
    Book C is used by children aged 9 to 12;
    Book D is used by children aged 10 to 13.

To help to identify suitable children for the series and to place them on appropriate books optional screening tests have been provided in each book. These contain answers and suggested marking schemes. However these tests are seen as optional as the teacher's judgement together with children's responses will be a more reliable guide to suitable placement.

What is in the books?

The challenges in the books are intended to enrich both the breadth and depth of the curriculum. The books therefore contain:

- Challenging problems on topics the children will have learnt at school. The problems reinforce and consolidate these concepts and at the same time are challenging and require mathematical insight, ability and logical thought.
- Topics that broaden the mathematics curriculum, such as number theory, creative and recreational topics and topics that highlight the aesthetic aspect of mathematics.

The relationship between the topics covered and the National Curriculum can be seen in the table on the contents page. Many of the challenges cut across several areas of mathematics and only those that feature strongly are shown in the table. In many of the challenges the child's approach to the problems will determine the areas covered rather than the problems themselves. For instance a child may choose to solve a problem either numerically or algebraically. It is not, therefore, appropriate to match each challenge with clearly defined statements of attainment or levels of the National Curriculum. It is very important to note that all of the challenges involve Using and Applying Mathematics (ATI) – as is shown on the contents table – as this underpins all other areas of mathematics. Indeed it is through developing the ideas and skills involved in Using and Applying Mathematics that children will encounter the real power of mathematics and mathematical thinking and hence cultivate their mathematical talents.

Who can use this book?

Any child who is interested in mathematics, who enjoys doing challenging problems, who is ready to persevere with a problem and has ability in mathematics can use the book. Book C is designed for children aged 9 to 12 of above average ability. It would be advisable for most children under 11 to complete Book B (and perhaps book A, depending on ability) before commencing Book C, because of the built-in progression between the challenges. The book can be used by:

- an individual child at home;
- a group of able children working together in a normal classroom;
- a group of children who have been withdrawn from their normal classroom to be taught together on a regular basis.

Children should be actively encouraged to work together in groups of two or three and communicate their ideas to each other. If the book is used by a child at home, parents should encourage their child to discuss results and findings with them.

A guide to problem solving

The ability to solve problems is at the heart of mathematics. Problem solving is the process of applying previously learnt knowledge to new and unfamiliar situations and many pupils find it difficult. Young children need to be introduced to strategies for solving problems. They may not know how to work systematically, how to draw up a table, look for a pattern or use a guess and check method, unless they meet these strategies. Many of the problems in this book suggest several different types of approaches and teachers should discuss the various strategies and help the children to see that one strategy may be more efficient than another.

The teacher's role in working through these challenges is vital if they are to help children reach their potential as mathematical thinkers. They must adopt a positive and supportive role to children's work and avoid providing quick and easy answers for the children. The children's struggle with the challenges is a valuable part of the activities, although there comes a point when a child may need more direct help to avoid frustration. A way to start some work is to say: 'let's find out......'. A way to encourage future work in the middle of a session to say: 'I wonder what would happen if. . .?'. It is most important that teachers emphasise the process of solving problems and not the product – that is, stress how a problem is solved, not just what the correct answer is. An emphasis on process, enables all pupils to experience some success in problem solving and the effort rather than the answer should be rewarded as much as possible in these activities.

Useful strategies in problem solving

TO START, UNDERSTAND THE PROBLEM
Read the problem carefully, possibly two or three times. Find the important relevant information and organise it into a table or draw a diagram. Decide what you are looking for.

EXPLORE AND DECIDE ON A PLAN
Think about all the different problem solving strategies that can be used:
draw up a table
use guess and check
look for a pattern
work systematically
make an organised list

eliminate possibilities
look for a simpler problem of the same type
use easier numbers
work backwards
draw a picture or diagram
make a model, act it out or use some concrete material

STUCK?
Ask yourself the following questions:
What is the given information and what am I looking for?
Is there enough or too much information?
Have I used all the relevant information?
What strategies might be helpful?
What relevant knowledge can I use?
Would it help to divide the problem into several parts?
Have I assumed (unconsciously) something that is incorrect?
When really stuck do something else and come back to the problem later with a fresh mind.

FINISHED?
Does the answer make sense and is the solution realistic?
Have you answered the question?
Should there be one solution or several?
Is it possible to do the problem in another and possibly more elegant way?
Compare your method with the methods used by other learners, and be ready to accept and appreciate different methods.
Reflect on the problem done. Think about the method you have used. Have you learnt something new? How alike or different was this problem from others that you have done? If you were stuck, what was your stumbling block?
Can you make up and solve a similar problem?

What should teachers do when children say they can't do a problem?
How and when should the teacher intervene? It is most important to find out if the learner has understood the ideas or concepts involved in the problem. Would some concrete material, diagram or a calculator be a help? Help children by asking questions that stimulate their thinking such as:
'Tell me what you are doing?'
'Think about why. . .?'
'What would happen if. . .?'
Intervention should be such that the child is able to progress and is not frustrated unduly. However, we must not rob the children of the joy and glory associated with struggle followed by success.

Qualities that should be rewarded and encouraged in problem solving
Perseverance – it means not giving up too easily.
Willingness to try and to take a risk – it is often not possible to write the answer immediately, so children will need to experiment and to explore before a solution becomes apparent. Making mistakes and getting stuck is a necessary and expected part of learning and improving thinking. Errors should be identified but used positively.
Children should be encouraged to see their errors and stumbling blocks as important and precious experiences that will contribute to their future learning.
Flexibility – If one approach fails learners will try a different approach.
Active involvement physical and mental – The use of concrete materials to develop the learning of abstract ideas and drawing diagrams should be encouraged.
Explanation, discussion and presentation – Children should discuss their work with others and record and report their ideas with as much explanation as possible.
Ability to make predictions – Having discovered a pattern by using a number of cases, the able child can extend the pattern and finally make a prediction.
Reflection – It is most important to encourage children to reflect back on a problem after having solved it, and to think about their own thinking. They should be ready to explain why they did what they did.

Some important considerations

Group work

'A growing body of research points to the benefits of having children learn in small co-operative groups. When children work in co-operative groups, the active participation of each child is maximised. Also many children feel more comfortable in small group settings and are therefore more willing to explain their ideas, speculate, question and respond to the ideas of others. In small co-operative groups students' opportunities to learn with understanding are supported and enhanced.' (May 1988 *The Arithmetic Teacher*, NCTM) However, having said all this, if a child wishes to work alone then she/he should not be forced to work in a group.

Investigative approaches

Some of the challenges in the books are presented in open-ended or investigative situations. The important aspects of mathematical investigations are:

1. There are no known outcomes at the beginning.

2. Learners get to formulate their own questions and explore different possibilities. They have to ask 'what would happen if. . .?'

3. Each child or group will explore a problem at their level of ability. Most problems can be investigated with a varying degree of sophistication. The same problem can thus be a challenge to children of a wide range of both age and ability.

Concrete material

Concrete material such as interlocking cubes, geoboards, balances and various grid and dot papers needs to be available for children to use as this makes learning much more enjoyable and meaningful for the child.

Dave Baker
Diana Brightling-Reed

Part 1: Screening Test Book C

Name: _____

Class: _____

1 I am thinking of two numbers. When I add them the sum is 9, and when I multiply them the product is 20.

My numbers are . . . .

2 I think of a number, double it, add 8 to the result and my answer is 22.

My number is . . . .

3 Daniel and his sister, Malika, collect marbles. Malika has 3 more marbles than Daniel, and together they have 19.

How many marbles does Daniel have? . . . .

4 What are the missing numbers in this pattern?

2	5	7	9	4	☐
↓	↓	↓	↓	↓	↓
3	9	13	17	☐	11

5 The numbers in these lines form patterns. In each line, write down the three numbers that will continue the pattern.

(a) 2, 4, 7, 11, 16 . . . .
(b) 1, 2, 4, 8 . . . .

6 In the following equations, the letters represent digits. What is the value of each letter?

(a) $C \times C = C + C$ C =
(b) $D + D + D + D = 24$ D =
(c) $M + M + M = 0$ M =
(d) $N \times N \times N = 1$ N =
(e) $P \times P + 3 = 19$ P =
(f) $17 - Q = 12$ Q =

7 How many squares can you find in this figure?

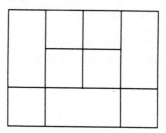

8 What numbers should be in the empty squares to give a product of 48?

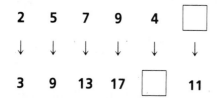

Write down as many solutions as you can.

9 If ○ $\underset{\triangle}{\rule{2cm}{0.4pt}}$ ★★★ and ★○○○ $\underset{\triangle}{\rule{2cm}{0.4pt}}$ ☐☐,

how many ★'s are needed to balance one ☐?

? $\underset{\triangle}{\rule{2cm}{0.4pt}}$ ☐

10 I have 3 piles of coins, and there are 19 coins altogether. The third pile has:
● twice as many coins as the first;
● one more coin than the second.

How many coins are in each pile?
It will help you to use this table.

First pile	Second pile	Third pile

11 Robbie has to number 67 seats for a concert. He sticks digits from 0 to 9 on the backs of the seats, so seat 25 will need one digit 2 and one digit 5.

(a) How many digit 3's will he need? . . . . .

(b) How many digits will he need altogether? . . . . .

12 In the expression ☐ ★ △, the symbol ★ means 'Double the first number and to the result add the second number'. For example:

$4 ★ 3 = 2 × 4 + 3$
$= 8 + 3$
$= 11$

Find the value of 3 ★ 4. . . . . .

13 I can buy 3 pens for £2.40.

(a) How many can I buy for £3.20? . . . . .

(b) How much will 7 pens cost? . . . . .

14 Mayan numerals consisted of dots and strokes representing the numbers up to twenty.

4 was ● ● ● ●

5 was ———

6 was ●
———

17 was ● ●
═══ (5 + 5 + 5 + 2)

(a) Write the number 13 as a Mayan numeral.

. . . .

(b) What does ● ● ● ——— represent? . . . . .

15 How many cubes make up this solid figure? . . . .

1 cube

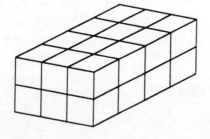

16 Miss Sport wants to conduct a tennis tournament for 12 outstanding students. Two people play in each match and each person plays until he or she loses. How many matches will be needed to decide a winner?

17 Mrs Clever used 14 posts when she fenced off her rectangular paddock. If the longer side has 1 more post than the shorter side, how many posts are on each short side?

18 Find the values of the letters A, B, C and D if the sum of each row and column is given. The value of letter E is 3, and the only other numbers that have been used are 1, 2, 4 and 5.

D	A	C	8
E	C	D	10
B	D	E	9
9	8	10	

19 At a country market, 3 peaches are worth 5 apricots and 2 apricots are worth 5 apples. Find how many apples I can trade for 6 peaches.

20 Bananas cost 40p for 1 lb and strawberries costs 50p for 1 lb. How many pounds of each did I buy, if I spent £2.60 and had 6 lb of fruit?

Screening Test: Solutions

1 5, 4 Use guess and check.

2 7 Work backwards: the number before adding 8 was 14, and before doubling was 7.

3 8 (Malika has 11) Use guess and check or act it out.

4

4	6
↓	↓
7	11

The pattern is 'Double the first number, then subtract 1'.

5 (a) 22, 29, 37 (b) 16, 32, 64

6 (a) C = 2 or 0 (b) D = 6 (c) M = 0 (d) N = 1
(e) P = 4 (f) Q = 5

7 12; 6 small (1×1), 4 medium (2×2), 2 large (3×3)

8 $24 \times \atop 2$ $16 \times \atop 3$ $12 \times \atop 4$ $48 \times \atop 1$

9 ★★★
★★★
★★★★ ☐☐ $\triangle$ → ★★★★★ ☐ $\triangle$

10 First: 4, second: 7, third: 8 Use guess and check.

11 (a) 17 For seat numbers 3, 13, 23, 30, 31–9, 43, 53, 63

(b) 125 $\frac{1 \qquad 9}{9} + \frac{10 \qquad 19}{20} + \frac{20 \qquad 29}{20}$

$\frac{30 \qquad 39}{20} + \frac{40 \qquad 49}{20} + \frac{50 \qquad 59}{20}$

$+ \frac{60 \qquad 67}{16}$

12 10(= 2 × 3 + 4)

13 (a) 4 pens (b) £5.60

14 (a) ••• (b) 8

15 24 cubes

16 11

17 A diagram is useful to show that there are 5 posts on the length and 4 posts on the width, but since the corner posts must not be counted twice there are only 14 posts. There are 4 posts on the short side.

18 A = 1, B = 4, C = 5, D = 2

19 6 peaches are worth 10 apricots, and 10 apricots are worth 25 apples. So 6 peaches can be traded for 25 apples.

20 Can be done by trial and error: 4 lb of bananas and 2 lb of strawberries (cost = 4 × 40 + 2 × 50 = £2.60)

Screening Test: Marking Scheme

1 2

2 2

3 2

4 2

5 (a) 1 (b) 1

6 (a) $\frac{1}{2}$ (b) $\frac{1}{2}$ (c) $\frac{1}{2}$
(d) $\frac{1}{2}$ (e) $\frac{1}{2}$ (f) $\frac{1}{2}$

7 2

8 2

9 2

10 2

11 (a) 2 (b) 2

12 2

13 (a) 2 (b) 2

14 (a) 1 (b) 1

15 2

16 3

17 3

18 3

19 3

20 3

Total Marks 50
If a student's total score is:
    less than 30, he/she should do Book B first.
    greater than 30, he/she can use this book.
    greater than 45, that is an excellent score!

What's the value?

Each figure in these equations stands for one of the digits 1 to 9.
Which is which?
 This is a difficult problem — can you solve it?

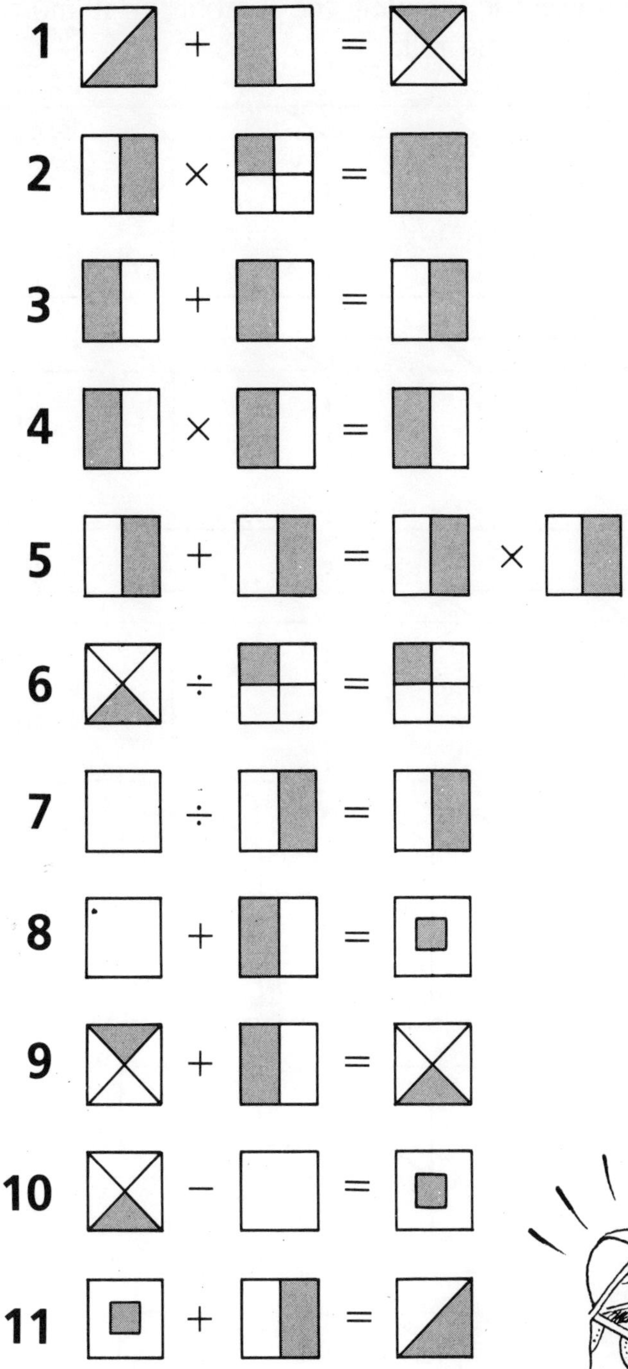

1 ◨ + �yl = ⊠

2 ◧ × ⊞ = ■

3 ◧ + ◧ = ◧

4 ◧ × ◧ = ◧

5 ◪ + ◨ = ◨ × ◧

6 ⊠ ÷ ⊞ = ⊞

7 □ ÷ ◨ = ◨

8 □ + ◧ = ▣

9 ⊠ + ◧ = ⊠

10 ⊠ − □ = ▣

11 ▣ + ◧ = ◩

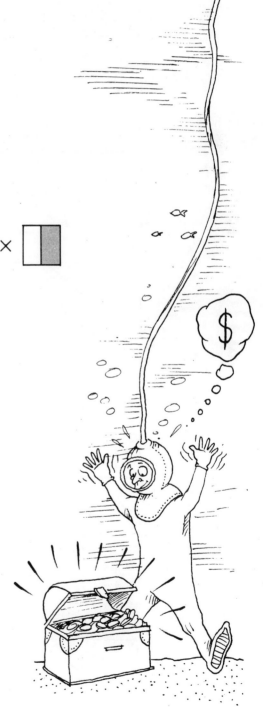

Rolling boxes

Boxes of various shapes have to be moved to a different position by turning them end over end, not by pushing or sliding them.

Can you place the symbols in the positions they will have each time a box is turned? Experiment by cutting out a box shape for each exercise, drawing the symbols on it and turning the shape as the box would roll.

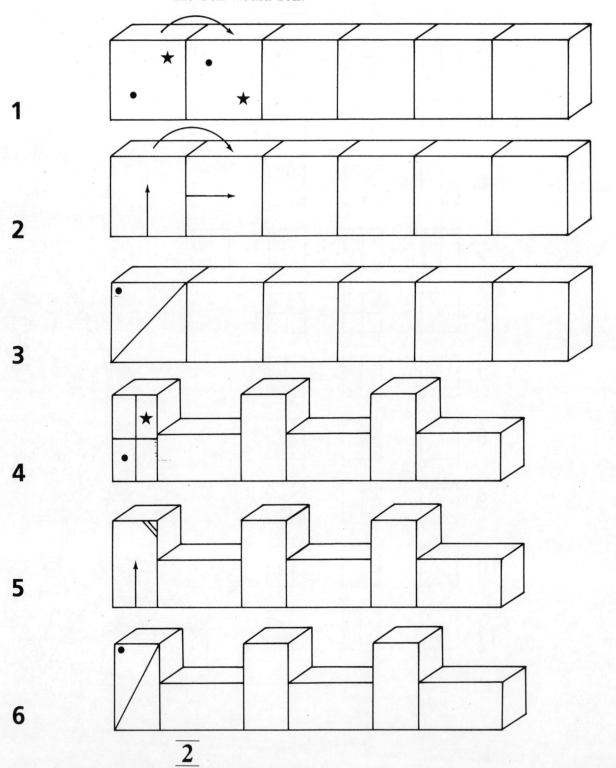

1

2

3

4

5

6

© Mathematics Enrichment Book C Simon & Schuster Education 1993

Find my rule

In each set of boxes, every box follows the same rule. Find the rule, write it down, and then work out which numbers are missing.

1 | 2 8 15 | | 5 20 27 | | 4 16 23 | | 3 |

2 | 9 2 12 | | 12 5 30 | | 10 3 18 | | 10 |

3 | 11 8 72 | | 7 4 36 | | 5 2 18 | | 9 |

4 | 8 4 9 | | 10 5 10 | | 12 6 11 | | 6 |

5 | 3 24 13 | | 5 40 29 | | 2 16 5 | | 6 |

6 | 4 36 31 | | 7 63 58 | | 3 27 22 | | 5 |

7 | 7 3 21 | | 9 5 35 | | 8 4 28 | | 6 |

8 | 9 3 24 | | 12 4 32 | | 21 7 56 | | 6 |

9 | 28 7 35 | | 12 3 15 | | 20 5 25 | | 16 |

10 | 7 42 21 | | 9 54 27 | | 2 12 | | 8 |

Make up one of your own for someone else to solve.

Digits and numbers

Can you work out and write down:

1 The largest 4-digit number that has 5 as one of its digits.

2 The smallest 4-digit number that has 5 as one of its digits.

3 The smallest 4-digit number.

4 The largest 5-digit number.

5 The smallest 4-digit number in which no digit is repeated.

6 The largest 4-digit number in which no digit is repeated.

7 The largest 4-digit number that contains the digits 2 and 7 and in which no digit is repeated.

8 The largest 3-digit number that uses the three smallest prime numbers.

9 The smallest 3-digit number that uses the three smallest prime numbers.

10 The smallest 4-digit number that has one 0 digit.

11 The largest 4-digit number that has one 0 digit.

12 The smallest 5-digit number.

13 The smallest 5-digit number in which the digit 0 is not used.

14 The largest 5-digit number in which the digits 9, 7 and 6 are not used.

15 The largest 4-digit number that has one 0 digit and in which no digit is repeated.

Picture graphs

These graphs give us information by means of pictures.

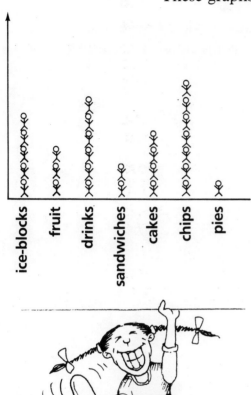

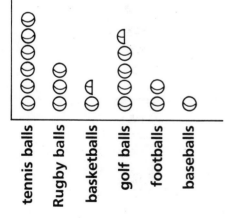

1 The picture graph opposite shows the number of children who bought various items at the snackbar.

Each ⚲ represents 3 children, and each child bought only one item.

(a) How many children bought a drink?

(b) How many children bought an ice-block?

(c) How many children bought a piece of cake?

(d) Which item was the most popular? How many children bought it?

(e) Which item was the least popular? How many children bought it?

(f) Altogether, how many children were served?

(g) If 15 sandwiches were prepared, how many were left over?

2 This picture graph shows the number of balls sold in one week by a sports shop. Each ⊖ represents 4 balls.

(a) How many of each of these balls were sold?
  (i) tennis balls
  (ii) footballs
  (iii) basketballs
  (iv) golf balls

(b) How many balls were sold altogether?

3 What else could you find out from these graphs? Make up some questions of your own and answer them.

Problem solving: Guess and check

1 Arrange the numbers from 1 to 7 in the circles of each figure so that the sum along each line is the number given below the figure.

(a)
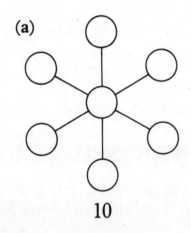
10

(b)
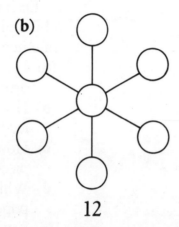
12

(c)
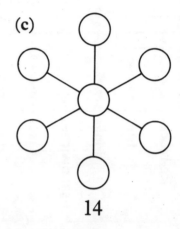
14

Hint: Try 1 in the centre.

2 Arrange the numbers from 1 to 9 in the circles of each figure so that the sum along each line is the number given below the figure.

(a)
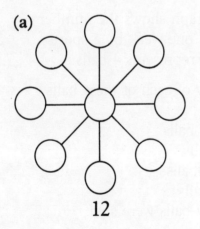
12

(b)
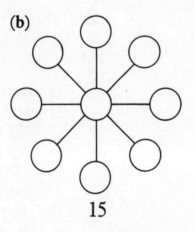
15

(c)
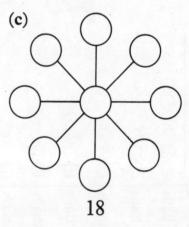
18

Hint: Try 1 in the centre.

3 Can you arrange the numbers so that other totals can be made? Explain.

6

© Mathematics Enrichment Book C Simon & Schuster Education 1993

Problem solving: Working systematically 1

1 Can you colour these flags in six different ways, using the colours red, blue and yellow, if each colour can be used only once on each flag?

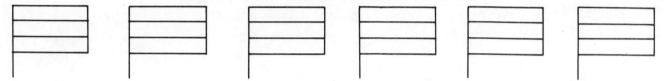

2 Using flags with three stripes, as in question 1, how many different combinations can you make with the colours red, blue and yellow if each colour can be used once, twice or three times in each flag?

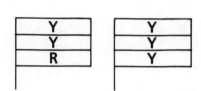

Two possible combinations are shown at left.

3 On the diagrams below, show that there are ten different paths that Edward can take from his home to his school, five blocks away. One possible route is drawn for you.

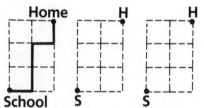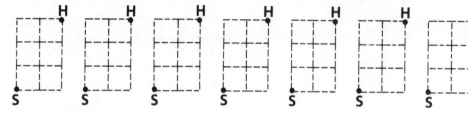

4 Gloria decides to make a circular bracelet for herself by threading three red and three white beads on a string. How many different patterns of red and white can she make?

Here is one possibility:

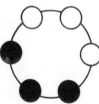

The bracelet can be turned around and these two patterns can be considered to be the same as the first. What do you think?

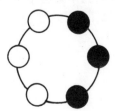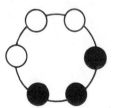

How many?

Remember to work systematically in answering these questions. For example, to find the total number of triangles in the figure at left, you could:

first count all the single triangles : 5
next look for double triangles (in this case, none) : 0
then count the large triangles (shown below) : 5
_____
10

1 How many triangles are there in this star?
Don't forget to count the single little triangles, the middle-sized triangles and the large triangles. A useful grid is on page 87.

2 **(a)** How many different line segments can be drawn to connect these four dots?

 (b) How many different line segments can be drawn to connect these five dots?

3 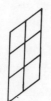 How many parallelograms can you find in the figure at left? There is a useful grid on page 87.

Don't forget to count first the small parallelograms and then those that are double (containing two), treble (containing three), quadruple (containing four) and large (containing six).

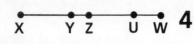

4 XY and XZ are two segments of this line. How many different line segments can you name?

5 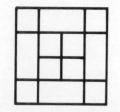 How many squares can you find in this figure? There is a useful grid on page 88.

© Mathematics Enrichment Book C Simon & Schuster Education 1993

What is my message?

In these messages, the letters have been replaced with numbers. Discover what they say, using the set of problems below each one as a key to the code.

1 $\overline{1\,8\,3\,5\,7}'\quad\overline{1\,8\,2\,2}\quad\overline{4\,0}\quad\overline{6\,9\,7}$

$L \times L = L + L$ $C + L = K$ $K \div K = R$

$R \times R = R$ $C^2 = U$ $L \times S = S$

$R + R = L$ $L^2 = I$ $N \times K = CK$

$C - L = R$ $L \times I = O$ $IU \div N = N$

$C \times L = F$ $F - F = S$

2 $\overline{4\,9\,1\,8\,7}\quad\overline{3\,7}\quad\overline{6\,2\,5\,5\,6}$

$M \div M = T$ $Y \times Y = IY$

$T \times T = T$ $T + U = I$

$I^2 = A$ $A - K = M$

$U^2 = M$ $MK \div K = A$

$K \times K = UK$ $IU \div H = M$

$$\begin{array}{r} THIS \\ IS \\ \hline THSM \end{array} +$$

$$\begin{array}{r} AM \\ AM \\ AM \\ \hline UHU \end{array} +$$

3   Try to make up
your own coded message.

Multiplication table squares

You may have been asked to complete multiplication table squares like square number 1.

Now, the challenge in numbers 2 to 8 is to find some of the numbers that have to be multiplied as well as to complete the squares. The missing numbers that have to be multiplied are all less than 12.

1

×	3	5	4	7
2	6	10	8	
8	24			
3				
9				

2

×	4	6	↗	
5			10	
↗		18		21
↗	32			
				12

You can start square 2 by filling in any of the spaces marked with an arrow.

3

×		3		
	4		18	
		24		
7	14			35
		36		

4

×		4		
	14		22	
		12		15
9	63			
			44	

5

×		8		
			20	40
		40		
3			15	
	27			90

6

×			7	
3				24
		16	56	
	54	12		
		18		

7

×		4		
		4	8	
	30		48	
	45		54	
		16		

8

×		2		
	25			
8				64
		6		
		100		

How does it start?

What numbers belong in the START circles of these flow charts? Here is an example:

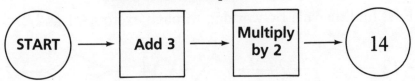

Begin with the final number and work backwards (that is, use the inverse of each operation).

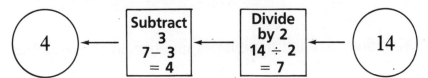

You could now check this solution like this:

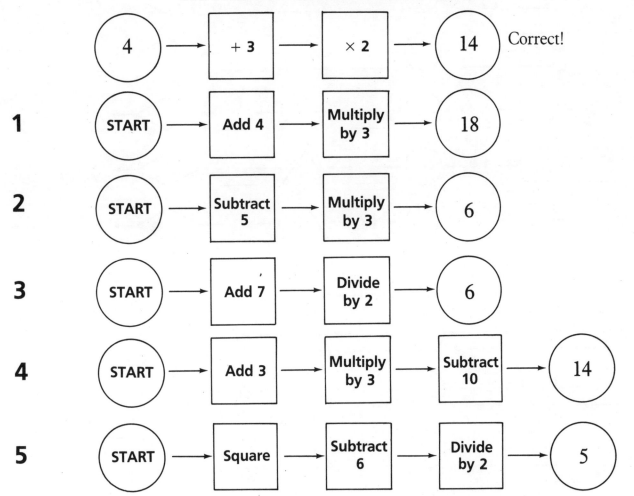

6   Try changing some of the end numbers. Can a number always be found for the start?

Missing numbers

All these exercises follow the same rule.

First find the rule by working through exercises 1 and 2.

1 4 → ☐ → 12 → ◯ → 24 → △ → 14 → ◇ → 7

2 7 → ☐ → 15 → ◯ → 30 → △ → 20 → ◇ → 10

Using this rule, find the missing numbers in exercises 3 to 12.

3 9 → ☐ → __ → ◯ → __ → △ → __ → ◇ → 12

4 10 → ☐ → __ → ◯ → __ → △ → __ → ◇ → __

5 12 → ☐ → __ → ◯ → __ → △ → __ → ◇ → __

6 __ → ☐ → 13 → ◯ → __ → △ → __ → ◇ → __

7 __ → ☐ → __ → ◯ → 18 → △ → __ → ◇ → __

8 __ → ☐ → __ → ◯ → __ → △ → 50 → ◇ → __

9 __ → ☐ → __ → ◯ → __ → △ → 42 → ◇ → __

10 __ → ☐ → __ → ◯ → __ → △ → 36 → ◇ → __

11 __ → ☐ → __ → ◯ → __ → △ → __ → ◇ → 20

12 __ → ☐ → __ → ◯ → __ → △ → __ → ◇ → 32

© Mathematics Enrichment Book C Simon & Schuster Education 1993

Number squares 1

Find the values of the letters A, B, C, D and E in these squares. The sum of each row and column is given, and only the numbers 1, 2, 3, 4, 5 and 6 have been used. Starting with the one letter-value given for each square, you will be able to work out the others.

1

D	A	C	12
E	C	D	11
B	D	E	8
8	12	11	

A B C D E
                2

Hint: Only the numbers 1, 2, 3, 4 and 5 have been used in this square.

			12
2			11
		2	8
8	12	11	

2

D	A	E	6
B	C	E	11
A	D	B	8
8	9	8	

A B C D E
1

	1		6
			11
1			8
8	9	8	

3

E	B	A	12
D	A	C	6
C	E	D	7
7	12	6	

A B C D E
3

		3	12
	3		6
			7
7	12	6	

4

A	D	E	9
F	B	C	12
E	F	B	9
12	7	11	

A B C D E F
5

5			9
			12
			9
12	7	11	

5

D	C	A	10
A	B	E	9
B	A	F	10
11	6	12	

A B C D E F
             4

			10
		4	9
			10
11	6	12	

13

Investigating magic squares

A square is said to be magic when the numbers in all horizontal, vertical and diagonal lines have the same sum.

8	1	6
3	5	7
4	9	2

This is an example of a magic square. It has a magic sum of 15, which is the sum of the numbers in all horizontal, vertical and diagonal lines.

10	3	8
5	7	9
6	11	4

1 Add 2 to each number in the example square above, giving this new square on the left. Is it still magic?

2 Now add 10 to each number in the example square above. Is it still magic?

3 Investigate what happens to the example square when you:
(**a**) subtract 1 from each number;
(**b**) multiply each number by 2;
(**c**) multiply each number by 3, 5 or 10;
(**d**) divide each number by 2;
(**e**) add $\frac{1}{2}$ to (or subtract $\frac{1}{2}$ from) each number.
Is the square still magic in each case? Explain.

1	14	7	12
15	4	9	6
10	5	16	3
8	11	2	13

4 Investigate what happens to this 4 × 4 magic square when to each number you:
(**a**) add 1, 2, 3, 10 or any number;
(**b**) subtract 1, $\frac{1}{2}$;
(**c**) multiply by 2, 3, 10 or any number;
(**d**) divide by 2.

Is the square still magic in every case?
Try to explain your answer.

© Mathematics Enrichment Book C Simon & Schuster Education 1993

Completing the lines

1 Can you make these squares, in which some numbers are missing, into magic squares? Work out which numbers you must put in the empty boxes so that all lines — horizontal, vertical and diagonal — will have the same total. You must first find each magic sum.

(a)

			10
14	9	8	3
12		2	
1	4		

(b)

8		2	
	5		3
	4	9	
1		7	12

(c)

8	15		5
	11		4
	6	7	
	10	3	

(d)

33	5		27
11		21	
	15		
9	29		3

(e)

23		10	20
12	18		
16	14	13	
11			

2 Complete each square grid below so that one — *and only one* — of the digits 1, 2, 3, 4 and 5 appears in each row, column or diagonal line.

(a)

1	3	5	2	4
5	2			
4	1			
3				

(b)

1	2	3	4	5
3	4	5		
5	1			

Largest and smallest

In these number sentences, $\square$ is a one-digit number (such as 5 or 6), while $\square\,\square$ is a two-digit number (such as 34 or 78).

Choosing any of the digits 1, 2, 3, 4, 5, 6, 7, 8 and 9, and using each one only *once* in a number sentence, fill in the small squares and complete the sentences so that:

1 You have the *largest* possible answer.

(a) $\square + \square =$
(b) $\square + \square + \square =$
(c) $\square + \square + \square + \square =$
(d) $\square - \square =$
(e) $\square + \square - \square =$
(f) $\square - \square - \square =$
(g) $\square\,\square =$
(h) $\square\,\square + \square =$
(i) $\square\,\square - \square =$
(j) $\square\,\square + \square\,\square =$
(k) $\square\,\square - \square\,\square =$
(l) $\square\,\square - \square\,\square - \square =$

2 You have the *smallest* possible answer (positive or zero).

(a) $\square + \square =$
(b) $\square + \square + \square =$
(c) $\square + \square + \square + \square =$
(d) $\square - \square =$
(e) $\square + \square - \square =$
(f) $\square - \square - \square =$
(g) $\square\,\square =$
(h) $\square\,\square + \square =$
(i) $\square\,\square - \square =$
(j) $\square\,\square + \square\,\square =$
(k) $\square\,\square - \square\,\square =$
(l) $\square\,\square - \square\,\square - \square =$

There are several possible solutions to some parts of group 2. Can you find them all? Why are there several solutions to some of them?

Remember to work systematically and also to use a digit only once in each sentence.

© Mathematics Enrichment Book C Simon & Schuster Education 1993

Multiplying puzzles

Try using a calculator to work out these problems. In each one, a digit can be used *once* only.

1 Using the digits 1, 2, 3 and 4, complete these exercises in such a way that your answer is as large as possible.

(a)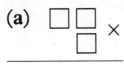

(b)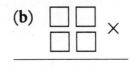

2 Arrange the digits 2, 4, 7, 8 and 9 in these boxes so as to get the largest possible product.

(a)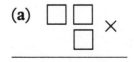

(b)

(c)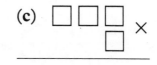

3 In each of these problems, place any three different digits to make a true statement. How many different solutions can be found in each case?

(a)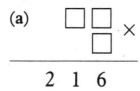

    2 1 6

(b)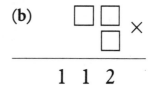

    1 1 2

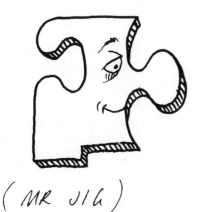

(MR JIG)

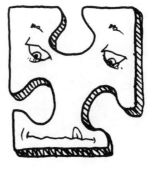

(MR SAW)

Counting cubes

Count the number of cubes that will be needed to build each of the towers below. To do this, first count the number of cubes in each layer, as set out in group 1. What patterns can you see?

1

(a)

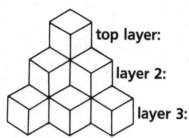

top layer:

layer 2:

Number of cubes:

(b)

top layer:

layer 2:

layer 3:

Number of cubes:

(c)

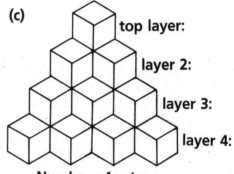

top layer:

layer 2:

layer 3:

layer 4:

Number of cubes:

2 (a)

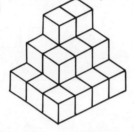

(b)

(c)

3 (a)

(b)

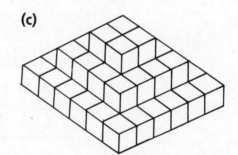

(c)

4 (a)

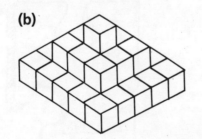

(b)

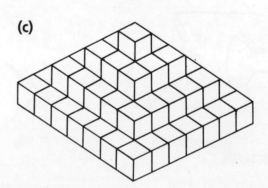

(c)

How can you check your answers?

Halves and quarters

This is half a shape: If you draw two of these on squared paper and cut them out, you can make the following whole shapes:

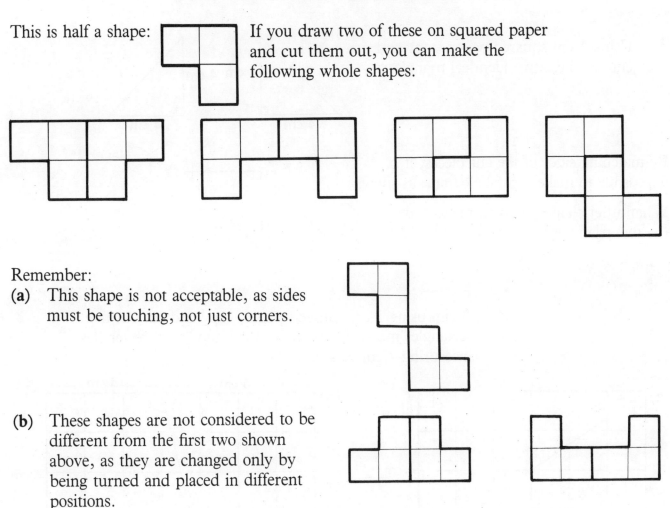

Remember:

(a) This shape is not acceptable, as sides must be touching, not just corners.

(b) These shapes are not considered to be different from the first two shown above, as they are changed only by being turned and placed in different positions.

1 Cut out two copies of each of the following half-shapes and join them in as many different ways as you can. Draw the shapes you make on squared paper.

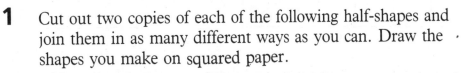

(a)   **(b)**   **(c)**

2 If the 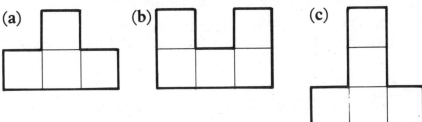 shape in the example and the three in exercise 1 are considered to be quarters, how many different whole shapes can you make?

   This time cut out four copies of each one, and don't forget to draw all the whole shapes on squared paper (see page 83).

Puzzles with shapes

1   Using 1 cm squared paper, copy and
cut out these two identical triangles:

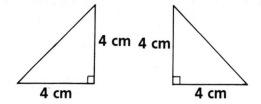

By matching sides of the cut pieces, it
is possible to make a parallelogram, as shown.

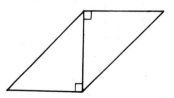

What other shapes can you make with
the two triangles?

2   Again using 1 cm squared paper, copy and cut out five
rectangles measuring 6 cm × 4 cm and seven rectangles
measuring 7 cm × 4 cm.

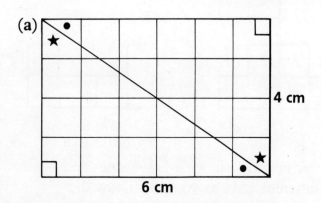

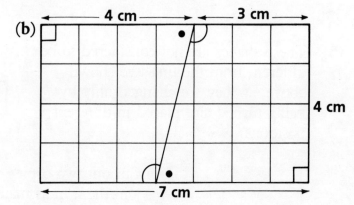

Cut all the 6 cm × 4 cm rectangles along
the diagonals, and by matching edges from
the cut pieces try to make five different
shapes.

Cut all the 7 cm × 4 cm rectangles along
an oblique line, as shown above, and by
matching edges from the cut pieces try to
make seven different shapes.

Glue all the different shapes in your book.

© Mathematics Enrichment Book C Simon & Schuster Education 1993

How many routes?

In the two diagrams below, how many different routes can you follow from A to B in each one if you go only in the direction of the arrows? Starting at A, count the number of different paths by which you can reach each circle, and write the numbers in the circles.

Here is an example:

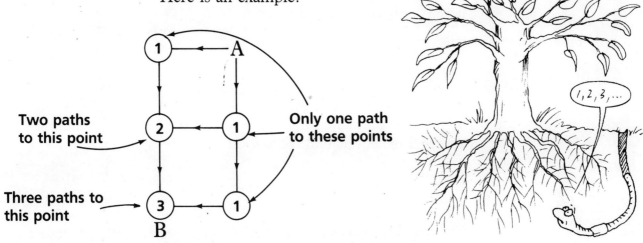

Two paths to this point

Only one path to these points

Three paths to this point

1, 2, 3, ...

Check the given possible routes carefully.

Copy each of the figures below, and when you have written the numbers in the circles, look for the pattern they make.

1

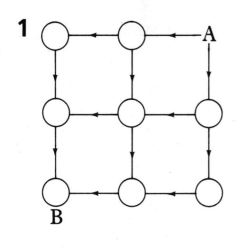

2

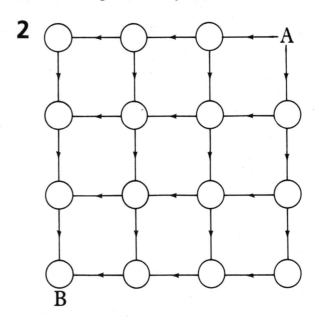

The pattern is called Pascal's triangle although it was used in China before he discovered it. Find out about Pascal's triangle.

Polyiamonds

Polyiamonds are the shapes that are formed when a number of congruent equilateral triangles (triangles all exactly the same shape) are joined together. They were given their name by a Glasgow mathematician, T.H.O'Beirne.

A *diamond* is formed by joining together two equilateral triangles. There is only one diamond.

There is also only one *triamond* — the shape formed by joining together three equilateral triangles.

There are three *tetriamonds*, which are formed by fitting together four equilateral triangles.

To answer the questions below, use isometric grid paper (page 86).

Be careful to note shapes which are the same, because each shape can be rotated (turned) or reflected (flipped) so that it looks different. For example, these shapes are the same as the last tetriamond shown above. Do you agree?

  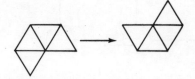

1 A *pentiamond* is formed by joining five equilateral triangles. How many pentiamonds can you find?

2 A *hexiamond* is formed by joining six equilateral triangles. How many hexiamonds can you find?

© Mathematics Enrichment Book C Simon & Schuster Education 1993

Strange maths symbols 1

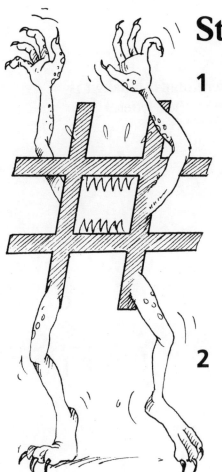

1 The symbol ★ placed between two numbers means that you should double the first number and add to the result half the second number.

$$7 \star 4 = 2 \times 7 + \tfrac{1}{2} \times 4 \quad \text{and} \quad 9 \star 2 = 2 \times 9 + \tfrac{1}{2} \times 2$$
$$\qquad\qquad = 14 + 2 \qquad\qquad\qquad\qquad = 18 + 1$$
$$\qquad\qquad = 16 \qquad\qquad\qquad\qquad\qquad = 19$$

Find the value of:
(a)	3 ★ 6	**(d)**	10 ★ 8
(b)	5 ★ 8	**(e)**	8 ★ 10
(c)	4 ★ 4	**(f)**	10 ★ 10

2 The symbol ⊙ placed between two numbers means 'square the first number and from your result subtract the second number'.

$$5 \odot 3 = 5^2 - 3 \qquad \text{and} \qquad 4 \odot 7 = 4^2 - 7$$
$$\qquad\quad = 25 - 3 \qquad\qquad\qquad\qquad = 16 - 7$$
$$\qquad\quad = 22 \qquad\qquad\qquad\qquad\qquad = 9$$

Find the value of these. In what way is (f) different?
(a)	3 ⊙ 6	**(d)**	10 ⊙ 8
(b)	5 ⊙ 8	**(e)**	8 ⊙ 10
(c)	4 ⊙ 4	**(f)**	1 ⊙ 4

3 The symbol # placed between two numbers means 'add these two numbers and divide the result by 2'.

$$5 \# 3 = (5 + 3) \div 2 \quad \text{and} \quad 8 \# 12 = (8 + 12) \div 2$$
$$\qquad\quad = 8 \div 2 \qquad\qquad\qquad\qquad = 20 \div 2$$
$$\qquad\quad = 4 \qquad\qquad\qquad\qquad\qquad = 10$$

Find the value of:
(a)	7 # 3	**(d)**	11 # 9
(b)	3 # 7	**(e)**	21 # 7
(c)	9 # 11	**(f)**	7 # 21

Now try putting these symbols between numbers of your choice. How could you ensure that your answers are always whole numbers?

Letter values

In the following exercises, the letters represent digits. No digit is repeated in any one exercise. Find the value of each letter.

1
$$
\begin{array}{r}
\text{B 1} \\
\text{B} \times \\
\hline
\text{2 B B}
\end{array}
$$

2
$$
\begin{array}{r}
\text{C 1} \\
\text{C} \times \\
\hline
\text{3 C C}
\end{array}
$$

3
$$
\begin{array}{r}
\text{4 A} \\
\text{A} \times \\
\hline
\text{2 7 A}
\end{array}
$$

4
$$
\begin{array}{r}
\text{M N} \\
\text{3} \times \\
\hline
\text{6 9}
\end{array}
$$

5
$$
\begin{array}{r}
\text{U V W} \\
\text{6} \times \\
\hline
\text{1 4 8 2}
\end{array}
$$

6
$$
\begin{array}{r}
\text{P} \\
\text{Q} + \\
\hline
\text{R R}
\end{array}
$$

7
$$
\begin{array}{r}
\text{D} \\
\text{E} \\
\text{F} + \\
\hline
\text{D F}
\end{array}
$$

8
$$
\begin{array}{r}
\text{J K} \\
\text{K} + \\
\hline
\text{K J}
\end{array}
$$

9
$$
\begin{array}{r}
\text{L G} \\
\text{L} + \\
\hline
\text{G H H}
\end{array}
$$

10
$$
\begin{array}{r}
\text{C D} \\
\text{C D} \\
\text{C D} \\
\text{C D} + \\
\hline
\text{E C}
\end{array}
$$

11
$$
\begin{array}{r}
\text{Y Y} \\
\text{W W} \\
\text{X X} + \\
\hline
\text{W X Y}
\end{array}
$$

12
$$
\begin{array}{r}
\text{P Q} \\
\text{P Q} \\
\text{Q P} + \\
\hline
\text{S S S}
\end{array}
$$

13
$$
\begin{array}{r}
\text{W T W} \\
\text{V W} - \\
\hline
\text{W T}
\end{array}
$$

14
$$
\begin{array}{r}
\text{L M N} \\
\text{L M N} \\
\text{L M N} + \\
\hline
\text{N N N}
\end{array}
$$

15
$$
\begin{array}{r}
\text{A A B} \\
\text{B B A} + \\
\hline
\text{B B B D}
\end{array}
$$

Problem solving: Working systematically 2

Working systematically through these problems will help you to account for all possibilities and avoid repetitions.

1 Four good friends — Robert, Yasu, Simon and Hassan — buy presents for each other for their birthdays.
(a) How many presents must each person buy?
(b) How many presents are bought altgether?

2 A family of five buy presents for each other. How many presents are bought altogether?

3 How many different three-letter code words can you make using the letters A, B and C:
(a) if repetition of the letters *is not* permitted;
(b) if repetition of the letters *is* permitted.

4 Three friends — Amanda (A), Michelle (M) and Sarah (S) are in a race at a carnival. List the number of different ways in which they could come first, second and third. (In your working, use their initials, as shown above.)

5 In how many ways can you put five fish in two bowls so that each bowl has at least one fish in it?

6 Winston goes away for the weekend and takes with him a blue and a yellow shirt, a navy and a white pair of shorts, and a black and a red jumper.
   How many different three-piece outfits can he make? Use a table like this to list the possibilities.

Shirts	Shorts	Jumpers

7 I have only a 2 g, a 5 g and a 10 g mass. How many different exact weights can I measure with these?

8 I have four 10p stamps and three 20p stamps. If I use one or more of these stamps, list the different amounts of postage I can make.

Problem solving: Working backwards

In each of these questions, I am thinking of a number. Examine the clues given, and then work backwards to find my numbers.

1 If you add 3 to the number and multiply the result by 2, you get 18.

2 If you double the number and then double the result, you get 20.

3 If you halve the number and then add 4, you get 10.

4 If you subtract 7 from the number and double the result, you get 12.

5 If you halve the number and then add 9, you get 14.

6 If you halve the number and double the result, you get 8.

7 If you double the number and halve the result, you get 6.

8 If you double the number and then subtract 4, you get 6.

9 If you add 6 to the number and then halve the result, you get 7.

10 If you subtract 3 from the number and multiply the result by 5, you get 30.

11 If you multiply the number by 5 and then subtract 3, you get 17.

12 If you halve the number and then halve the result, you get 4.

13 If you multiply the number by itself (square it), you get 16.

14 If you square the number and then add 1, you get 10.

15 If you subtract 4 and square the result, you get 16.

16 If you subtract 7, then square the result you get 4.

17 If you multiply the number by 9 and then add 3, you get 30.

18 If you square the number and then add 7, you get 23.

19 If you square the number, then add 2 and halve the result, you get 3.

20 Make up some of these of your own.

© Mathematics Enrichment Book C Simon & Schuster Education 1993

Problem solving: Act it out

1 Start with a 10p coin. How many other 10p coins can you fit around the outside of it?

   Now repeat this experiment with £1 coins, with 20p coins, with 5p coins and with any other coins. What pattern do you find?

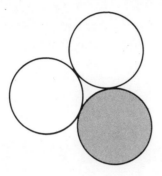

2 Catherine and Fiona receive a total of £25 pocket money each month.

   How much does each girl receive if:

   (a) Catherine has £1 more than Fiona?

   (b) Catherine has £3 more than Fiona?

   (c) Catherine has £5 more than Fiona?

3 Ten 5c coins are placed in a row on a desk.

   Every second coin is then replaced with a 10c coin.

   Every third coin is then replaced with a 20c coin.

   Every fourth coin is then replaced with a 50c coin.

   And finally, every fifth coin is replaced with a $1 coin.

   What is the value of the ten coins now on the desk?

Problem solving: Finding several solutions

1 Using 4 × 4 grid paper or squared paper, show the different ways in which you can place four crosses in a 4 × 4 square so that there is only one cross in any row or column.
Here is one possible way:

			X
		X	
X			
	X		

How many others are there?

2 Here is one way in which three shaded circles can be placed so that they all touch the circumference of the large circle: two touch inside and the third touches outside.
Draw clear diagrams to illustrate the other possibilities.

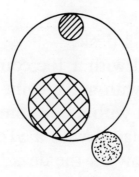

3 Geoffrey's house is 3 km from school, while Effie's house is 2 km from school.
Draw diagrams showing the possible positions of Effie's house, Geoffrey's house and the school.

© Mathematics Enrichment Book C Simon & Schuster Education 1993

Problem solving: Using tables 1

Draw up tables and use guess-and-check to solve these problems.

1 Esi and Marc collect marbles. Esi has 3 more marbles than Marc. Together they have 21.
How many marbles does each have?

Esi	Marc	Total marbles

2 Mrs Kind bought a total of 14 ice-creams and ice-lollies for her children and their friends. Ice-creams cost £1 each, while ice-lollies cost 50p each. If Mrs Kind spent £10 altogether, how many of each did she buy?

Ice-creams (£1)	Ice-lollies (50p)	Total spent

3 John has some 5p and 10p coins in his pocket.
Find out how many of each coin John has if:
(**a**) he has 40p altogether and a total of 6 coins;
(**b**) he has 80p altogether and a total of 11 coins;
(**c**) he has 45p altogether and a total of 6 coins;
(**d**) he has 70p altogether and a total of 8 coins;
(**e**) he has 50p altogether and a total of 8 coins.

5p coins	10p coins	Total coins	Total amount

Problem solving: With extra information

Sometimes in solving problems you may find you have more information than you need. In these exercises, you will have to work out which is the relevant data.

1 Ade weighed 44 kg; he weighed 12 kg more than Steve. Yoko weighed 9 kg more than Steve. How much did Steve weigh?

2 Four girls competed in the high jump at the school carnival. Layla, who is 13 years old, jumped 6 cm higher than Lisa. Lisa jumped 3 cm lower than Kate, but 2 cm higher than Zara. Zara and Lisa are cousins.
   If Kate jumped 95 cm, how high did the other three girls jump?

3 The same four girls also competed in the long jump.
   Layla jumped 5 cm further than Lisa and 8 cm further than Kate. Zara jumped 10 cm further than Lisa and 4 cm further than her best friend, Rhonda.
   If Kate jumped 252 cm, how far did the other girls jump?

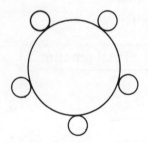

4 The Happy family — Mr Happy, Mrs Happy, Marc, Jenny and Grandma Happy — were sitting at their round kitchen table, having dinner.
   • Mrs Happy did not sit next to her husband.
   • Jenny sat next to her father.
   • Last night Jenny sat next to her brother and they had a fight.
   • Marc did not like the vegetable soup and did not feel too happy, as his mother was sitting next to him and made him eat it.
   • Grandma Happy sat next to her son and her grandson.
   • Jenny loved the cake Grandma made.
   Draw a diagram of the Happy family's seating arrangement.

© Mathematics Enrichment Book C Simon & Schuster Education 1993

Who am I?

To discover who I am, you must eliminate impossibilities.

1 I am the only even prime number.

2 I am the only number that is neither prime nor composite.

3 I am the only two-digit, odd composite number less than 20.

4 I am a two-digit number.
I am a square number.
I am greater than 29.
I am less than 42.

5 I am the sixth prime number.

6 I am a two-digit number.
I am less than 40.
I am exactly divisible by 3 and 10.

7 I am the smallest number exactly divisible by 2, 3 and 4.

8 I am a square number.
I am a two-digit number.
The sum of my digits is 7.
I am divisible by 5.

9 I am greater than 20 and less than 30.
I am even.
I am exactly divisible by 3.

10 I am a two-digit number, less than 25.
I am even.
The sum of my digits is 9.
I am exactly divisible by 3.

11 I am a two-digit number, less than 90 and greater than 45.
I am exactly divisible by 10 and 3.

12 I am a two-digit number.
The sum of my digits is 3.
I am exactly divisible by 5 and 2.

13 I am a two-digit number, less than 25.
I am exactly divisible by 2 and 7.

14 I am a two-digit number, less than 30.
I am exactly divisible by 6 and 8.

Now make up some clues for mystery numbers of your own choice.

Perimeter and area investigation

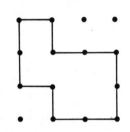

The *perimeter* of a figure is the distance around it.

The *area* of a figure is the amount of surface enclosed by it.

This figure has a perimeter of 12 units and an area of 6 square units.

WHAT'S THE DISTANCE?

1 In the table below, the perimeters and the areas of figures are given. Draw each of these figures on dot paper or construct them on a geoboard. A useful grid is on page 89.

The sides of all figures must be horizontal or vertical.

	Perimeter (units)	Area (square units)
(a)	4	1
(b)	6	2
(c)	8	4
(d)	10	4
(e)	10	5
(f)	12	5*
(g)	10	6
(h)	12	8
(i)	12	9
(j)	16	16

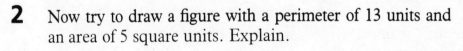

10 METRES!

* There are many possible solutions to (f). How many can you find?

2 Now try to draw a figure with a perimeter of 13 units and an area of 5 square units. Explain.

Growing squares and triangles

1 **(a)** Here is a square that is growing in size.

Work out the perimeter and the area of each size, and record your answers in your own way.

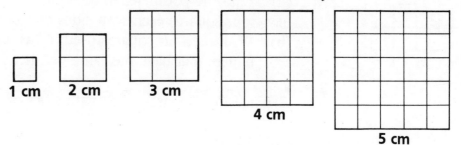

1 cm   2 cm   3 cm   4 cm   5 cm

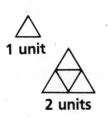

1 unit

2 units

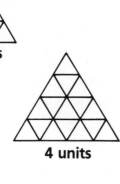

3 units

4 units

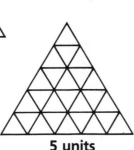

5 units

(b) Can you predict the perimeter and the area of squares whose sides are (a) 6 cm and (b) 10 cm?

2 An *equilateral* triangle is a triangle whose three sides are the same length.

(a) Here is an equilateral triangle that is growing in size.

Work out the perimeter and the area of each size, and record your answers. A table like the one below may be helpful.

 1 triangular grid

 Since 4 grids fit into this larger triangle, its area is 4 triangular grids.

Side (units)	Perimeter (units)	Area (triangular grids)
1	3	1
2	6	4
3		
4		
5		

(b) Can you predict the perimeters and the areas (measured in triangular grids) of equilateral triangles whose sides measure (a) 6 units and (b) 10 units?

Perimeter puzzles

Use squared paper to draw the figures in these exercises (see page 83).

1 (a) Find the perimeter of this figure, which is made up of four squares each with sides of 1 cm.

(b) With the four squares used in (a), can you draw other figures that have the same perimeter as the original one?

2 Arrange four squares, each with sides of 1 cm, to make a perimeter of:

(a) 14 cm

(b) 12 cm

(c) 10 cm

(d) 8 cm

Draw as many different figures as you can with each measurement.

3 The perimeter of a square field is 36 m. What is the length of each side?

4 The perimeter of a rectangular field is 60 m. If the length is twice the width, what is the length of the field?

5 The length of a rectangular field is three times the width and the perimeter of the field is 48 m. Find the length and the width.

6 Four square tables are pushed next to each other to form one large table. If the perimeter of the new large table is 20 m, what is the perimeter of one square table?

© Mathematics Enrichment Book C Simon & Schuster Education 1993

Palindromic numbers

MY NAME IS ANNA, FORWARDS AND BACKWARDS.

The numbers 121, 797 and 3443 are all examples of palindromic numbers, since they read the same both forwards and backwards.

It is very interesting that, starting with any two-digit number, you can make (generate) a palindromic number in the following way:

Start with a two-digit number   : 13

Reverse the digits   : 31

Add, to make a palindromic number : 44

These numbers required *one stage* to become palindromic.

Now start with this number   :47

Reverse the digits   :74

Add, to make a palindromic number : 121

However:

If you start with this number   : 39

Reverse the digits   : 93

This number is not yet palindromic.

and add   : 132

So you must repeat the process.

Reverse the digits   : 231

Add again   : 363

Number 39 took *two stages* to become palindromic.

1 Show that to become palindromic:
   (a) 59 requires three stages;
   (b) 78 requires four stages;
   (c) 79 requires six stages.

2 Investigate how many stages numbers less than 100 take to become palindromic. Are there any patterns?

3 'Noon' and 'madam' are examples of palindromic words. Write down as many palindromic words as you can find.

Shopping at a barter market

I'LL TRADE 3 TOMATOES FOR 3 PEARS.

Sometimes people swap goods for other goods, instead of using money. This kind of trading is called a barter system.

At one particular barter market:

10 potatoes = 5 apples = 2 tomatoes = 1 lettuce

which means that one lettuce can be traded for any of the first three items.

Therefore, 2 lettuces are worth 4 tomatoes or 10 apples or 20 potatoes.

1 If I have 3 lettuces, how many of each of the following can I trade for them?
   (a) tomatoes
   (b) apples
   (c) potatoes

2 How many lettuces will I need if I want to obtain these goods?
   (a) 10 tomatoes
   (b) 20 apples
   (c) 60 potatoes

3 Calculate how many apples I will need if I want to obtain:
   (a) 4 tomatoes
   (b) 20 tomatoes
   (c) 50 potatoes
   (d) 6 lettuces

4 If I have 25 apples, how many of each of the following can I trade for them?
   (a) lettuces
   (b) tomatoes
   (c) potatoes

5 If I have 10 tomatoes and 10 apples, how many lettuces can I trade for them?

6 If I want to obtain 16 tomatoes, how many of each of the following will I need to swap for them?
   (a) lettuces
   (b) apples
   (c) potatoes

36

© Mathematics Enrichment Book C Simon & Schuster Education 1993

Tree diagrams

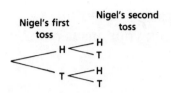

Here is an example of a tree diagram.

If Nigel is tossing a 10p coin, each toss can turn up either heads (H) or tails (T). When Nigel tosses the coin twice, the possible results are HH, HT, TH or TT.

A tree diagram can be very helpful in working out this type of problem. Read along the branches of the first diagram to give all the possibilities described.

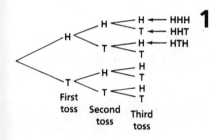

First toss Second toss Third toss

1 If Nigel tossed a coin three times, a tree diagram would look like the one at left.

Continue to write down all the possibilities.

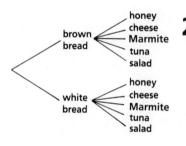

2 Every morning Malcolm makes his own sandwich. He can use brown or white bread and can choose between honey, cheese, Marmite, tuna or salad filling. Using the tree diagram on the left, work out the number of variations Malcolm can use.

3 Edwyn and Barry are planning to go to Brighton Marina. They can travel from home to the town by train, coach or car. From the town they can go to Brighton Marina by walking, catching a bus or taking a taxi.

List the various ways in which they can travel from home to Brighton Marina.

You can either draw a tree diagram *or* represent the information with a drawing.

Number patterns

The number sentences in each exercise follow a pattern. Find the pattern, continue it for a few more lines, and check your answer on a calculator.

1 $37 \times 3 = 111$
$37 \times 6 = 222$
$37 \times 9 = 333$

2 (a) $91 \times 1 = 91$
$91 \times 2 = 182$
$91 \times 3 = 273$
$91 \times 4 = 364$

(b) $9109 \times 1 = 9109$
$9109 \times 2 = 18\ 218$
$9109 \times 3 = 27\ 327$
$9109 \times 4 = 36\ 436$

3 $143 \times 7 = 1001$
$143 \times 14 = 2002$
$143 \times 21 = 3003$

4 $131 \times 11 = 1441$
$131 \times 111 = 14\ 541$
$131 \times 1111 = 145\ 541$

5 $101 \times 22 = 2222$
$101 \times 222 = 22\ 422$
$101 \times 2222 = 224\ 422$

6 $101 \times 33 = 3333$
$101 \times 333 = 33\ 633$
$101 \times 3333 = 336\ 633$

7 $37 \times 3 = 111$
$37 \times 33 = 1221$
$37 \times 333 = 12\ 321$

8 $1 \times 9 + 2 = 11$
$12 \times 9 + 3 = 111$
$123 \times 9 + 4 = 1111$

9 $9 \times 9 + 7 = 88$
$98 \times 9 + 6 = 888$
$987 \times 9 + 5 = 8888$

10 $1 \times 8 + 1 = 9$
$12 \times 8 + 2 = 98$
$123 \times 8 + 3 = 987$

11 $11^2 = 121$
$111^2 = 12\ 321$
$1111^2 = 1\ 234\ 321$

12 $3367 \times 33 = 111\ 111$
$3367 \times 66 = 222\ 222$
$3367 \times 99 = 333\ 333$

13 $37\ 037 \times 3 = 111\ 111$
$37\ 037 \times 6 = 222\ 222$
$37\ 037 \times 9 = 333\ 333$

14 $999\ 999 \times 2 = 1\ 999\ 998$
$999\ 999 \times 3 = 2\ 999\ 997$
$999\ 999 \times 4 = 3\ 999\ 996$

Number squares 2

Find the values of the letters A, B, C, D and E in these squares. The sum of each row and column is given, and only the numbers 1, 2, 3, 4 and 5 have been used. Starting with the one letter-value given for each square, you will be able to work out the others.

1

A	A	C	B	10
B	E	B	D	17
E	E	C	D	11
B	D	A	C	12
15	12	9	14	

A = 2

A   B   C   D   E

2

2	2			10
				17
				11
		2		12
15	12	9	14	

2

D	A	D	B	8
C	C	A	B	12
B	D	C	A	12
A	E	B	C	13
12	12	10	11	

A   B   C   D   E

C = 4

				8
4	4			12
		4		12
			4	13
12	12	10	11	

3

E	D	C	A	11
E	C	B	A	10
D	A	C	E	11
C	A	B	D	12
12	10	10	12	

A   B   C   D   E

E = 3

3				11
3				10
			3	11
				12
12	10	10	12	

4

B	B	D	C	15
D	D	A	C	13
E	A	C	E	9
E	C	B	D	14
15	12	12	12	

A   B   C   D   E

D = 5

		5		15
5	5			13
				9
			5	14
15	12	12	12	

Strange maths symbols   2

In these exercises, new signs have been introduced to represent various uses of the symbols ×, +, − and ÷. Each exercise follows a particular rule.

Here is an example:

$3 \boxtimes 2 = 25$ $2 \boxtimes 4 = 36$
$7 \boxtimes 1 = 64$ $1 \boxtimes 3 = ?$

This rule is 'Add the two numbers, then square the result (or multiply the result by itself); so that $\square \boxtimes \triangle = (\square + \triangle)^2$.

Therefore $1 \boxtimes 3 = (1 + 3)^2$
$\qquad\qquad\quad = 4^2$
$\qquad\qquad\quad = 16$

Find the rule in each exercise and complete the final number sentence.

1 $3 \odot 4 = 12$
$5 \odot 9 = 19$
$8 \odot 2 = 15$
$7 \odot 3 = ?$
Hint: Try adding.

2 $7 \wedge 2 = 7$
$9 \wedge 3 = 8$
$5 \wedge 1 = 6$
$6 \wedge 4 = 4$
$8 \wedge 2 = ?$
Hint: Try subtracting.

3 $5 \star 1 = 7$
$3 \star 4 = 11$
$1 \star 7 = 15$
$4 \star 3 = 10$
$6 \star 2 = ?$
Hint: Try doubling.

4 $6 \# 4 = 5$
$7 \# 1 = 4$
$3 \# 5 = 4$
$4 \# 2 = 3$
$3 \# 1 = ?$
Hint: Try adding.

5 $3 \heartsuit 2 = 1$
$5 \heartsuit 1 = 16$
$8 \heartsuit 2 = 36$
$7 \heartsuit 4 = 9$
$6 \heartsuit 1 = ?$
Hint: Try subtracting.

6 $7 \vee 2 = 18$
$1 \vee 5 = 12$
$3 \vee 2 = 10$
$6 \vee 4 = 20$
$2 \vee 4 = ?$
Hint: Try adding.

7 $8 \oslash 2 = 18$
$2 \oslash 8 = 12$
$3 \oslash 5 = 11$
$1 \oslash 3 = 5$
$4 \oslash 3 = ?$
Hint: Try doubling.

8 $8 \blacktriangle 3 = 7$
$4 \blacktriangle 2 = 4$
$6 \blacktriangle 6 = 9$
$2 \blacktriangle 7 = 8$
$10 \blacktriangle 2 = ?$
Hint: Try halving.

9   Now make up a challenge using a strange maths symbol of your own.

What is my question?

To solve these problems, you will need to know your tables very well. Study the example before you begin.

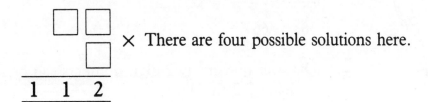 × There are four possible solutions here.

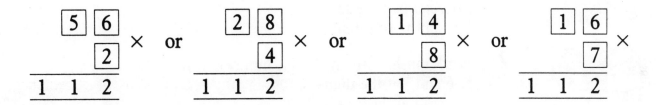

How many different solutions can you find for each of the problems below?

1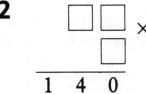

2

3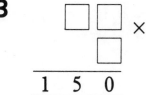

4

5

6

7

8

Digit puzzles

Using the digits 5 and 6, we can form two 2-digit numbers — 56 and 65 — if the digits cannot be repeated. However, if they can be repeated we can form these numbers:

55	65
56	66

1 Discover how many 2-digit numbers can be formed using 5, 6 and 7 if the digits
(a) cannot be repeated;
(b) can be repeated.
List all the possibilities.

2 Work out how many 3-digit numbers can be formed using 5, 6 and 7 if the digits
(a) cannot be repeated;
(b) can be repeated.

3 How many 4-digit numbers can be formed using 5, 6, 7 and 8 if the digits cannot be repeated?

4 (a) Luther has to number 27 seats for a concert by sticking the digits 0 to 9 on the back of the seats. Therefore, for seat 23 he will need one digit 2 and one digit 3.
   (i) How many digit 5's will he need?
   (ii) How many digit 2's will he need?
   (iii) How many digit 0's will he need?
(b) Luther now has to number 87 seats.
   (i) How many digit 5's will he need?
   (ii) How many digit 2's will he need?
   (iii) How many digit 0's will he need?

(3 LETTERS)

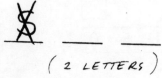

(2 LETTERS)

CAN YOU WORK OUT
THIS PUZZLE?

ANSWER: DIG PIT
DIGIT

© Mathematics Enrichment Book C Simon & Schuster Education 1993

Matchstick puzzles

In each exercise, use matchsticks to build the shapes that are given above the tables. Now continue the pattern, following the rule you have observed. Complete the table and say what you see. Use the pattern to predict the number of matches you would need for the tenth figure.

1

Number of triangles	1	2	3	4	5	→	10
Number of matches						→	

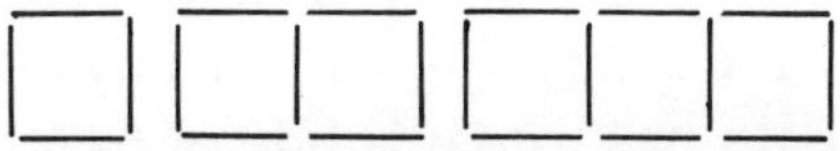

2

Number of squares	1	2	3	4	5	→	10
Number of matches						→	

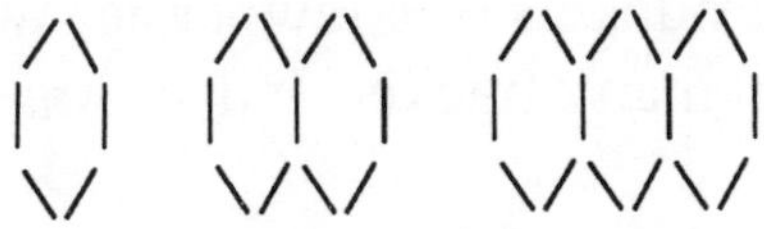

3

Number of hexagons	1	2	3	4	5	→	10
Number of matches						→	

4

Number of houses	1	2	3	4	5	→	10
Number of matches						→	

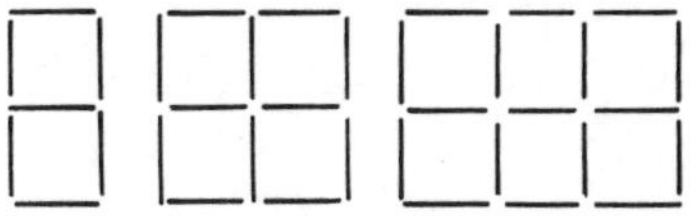

5

Number of double squares	1	2	3	4	5	→	10
Number of matches						→	

6 Make up a puzzle of your own.

Problem solving:
Your own strategy   1

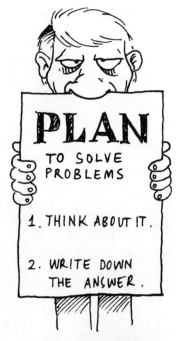

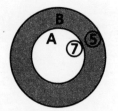

1 Nancy and Lucy each began reading *The Babysitters' Club* on Monday. Nancy reads 9 pages each day and Lucy reads 7 pages each day.

On what day of the week will Nancy finish reading 54 pages? What page will Lucy be finishing on that day?

2 When Ritu returned to the library the book she had borrowed, she read the following notice about fines:

If a book is 1 day overdue, the fine is 1p; for 2 days it is 2p, for 3 days, 4p, for 4 days, 8p, and so on.

If Ritu has to pay a fine of 64p, how many days overdue is her book?

3 Salma and Becky took a holiday job strawberry picking. Salma filled 4 buckets of strawberries while Becky filled 3 buckets.

How many buckets will Salma fill while Becky fills 24?

4 In a game of darts, a person can score 7 points if the dart lands in circle A, and 5 points if the dart lands in shaded area B.

Jim threw 3 darts to area A and 3 darts to area B. If Michael threw only one dart to area A and beat Jim by 1 point, how many of his darts landed in area B?

5 Mr and Mrs Healthy have 3 children. The oldest child drinks 1 pint of milk in 2 days. The two younger children together drink 3 pints of milk in 2 days, while the parents drink 1 pint of milk in 3 days.

How many pints of milk does the Healthy family drink in 6 days?

6 Heidi has some coins in her purse. She has twice as many 10p coins as 5p. She has one less 20p coin than she has 10p, and she has four 50p coins. The combined value of her 20p and 50p coins is £3.

How many coins of each value does Heidi have?

© Mathematics Enrichment Book C Simon & Schuster Education 1993

Problem solving: Your own strategy 2

1 Scott was given his pocket money on Sunday. On Monday he spent £2.50 on a present. On Tuesday he did some gardening and was paid £8. On Wednesday he bought a drink for 80p.

If Scott now has £9.20, how much pocket money was he given?

2 When Leah and her two children, Andrew and Ramah, stepped onto a scale, it showed 127 kg as their total weight. When Andrew got off the scale showed 103 kg, and when Ramah got off and Andrew stepped back on the scale it showed 89 kg.

How much did Leah and each of her two children weigh?

3 There are 35 people in a restaurant; 25 drink coffee and 14 drink lemonade. Everyone has either one or both of the drinks.

How many people had both?

4 Shing started reading a new novel. She read 11 pages on the first night, 9 pages on the second night, 7 pages on the third night and so on, continuing this pattern.

If the novel has 36 pages, how long will it take her to finish reading it?

5 Miranda bought some sweets and gave 4 of them to each of 3 friends. If she had 5 sweets left, how many did she buy?

6 Mrs Chong bought 5 ice-creams for £4 and 3 packets of chips for £3.60.

How much did each ice-cream cost?

7 Miss Major had 120 five pound tickets for the end-of-year concert. She sold a quarter of the tickets on the first day.

How many more tickets does Miss Major have to sell?

8 If 3 apples are worth 2 oranges, how many oranges are 12 apples worth?

9 I can buy 2 folders for £5. How many can I buy for £25?

10 I can buy 6 mugs for £18. How many mugs can I buy for (a) £9 and (b) £36?

Make a model, act it out

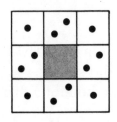

1 This diagram shows how 12 prisoners are arranged in 8 cells, with 4 prisoners in each row of 3 cells. Now arrange 9 prisoners in the 8 cells so that there are 4 in each row of three.

How many different solutions can you find?

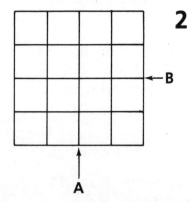

2 Amy is playing with building blocks. She has 4 large blocks ☐ and 4 small blocks ▨ . She places these 8 blocks on the board shown at left in such a way that each row contains one large and one small block and each column contains one large and one small block.

Using squared paper, show how Amy arranges the blocks so that the views (a), (b) and (c), shown below, would be seen if you look in the direction of the arrows.

(a)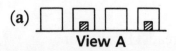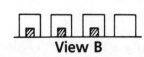

It is recommended that you draw up a large board, like the diagram above, and use blocks or jars.

Then draw your solution on 4 × 4 grid paper from page 85.

(b)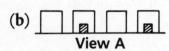

(c)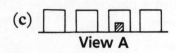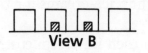

© Mathematics Enrichment Book C Simon & Schuster Education 1993

Measurement puzzles

You could use containers and water to act out these problems, or you could draw diagrams in your book for each one, stating carefully what you are doing at every stage. For example, you could start problem 1(a) like this:

Fill the 7 litre bucket with water.

1 The two buckets shown here are marked 7 litres and 3 litres. They have no other markings.

Show how these two buckets can be used to measure exactly:

(a) 4 litres of water;
(b) 1 litre of water;
(c) 2 litres of water;
(d) 5 litres of water;
(e) 9 litres of water.

2 These buckets are marked 5 litres and 3 litres. They have no other markings.

Show how the two buckets can be used to measure exactly 7 litres of water.

3 Make up a puzzle of your own.

Find my three numbers

In each exercise, I am thinking of three numbers: $\square$, $\triangle$ and $\bigcirc$.
Use the given clues to find my numbers.

1
$\triangle + \triangle + \triangle = 12$
$\triangle + \bigcirc = 7$
$\square + \square = \triangle$
$\triangle + \square + \bigcirc = 9$

2
$\square + \square = 18$
$\square \div \triangle = \triangle$
$\square - \triangle = \bigcirc$
$\triangle + \triangle = \bigcirc$

3
$\triangle + \triangle + \triangle = 18$
$\triangle \div \bigcirc = \square$
$\bigcirc + 1 = \square$
$\triangle - \bigcirc - \square = 1$

4
$\bigcirc + \bigcirc = 16$
$\triangle + \triangle = \bigcirc$
$\square - \triangle = 5$
$\square - \bigcirc = 1$

5
$\square + \square + \square + \square = \triangle + \triangle$
$\triangle - \square = 5$
$\triangle \div \square = 2$
$\triangle + \square + \bigcirc = 18$

6
$\triangle + \bigcirc = 8$
$\triangle - \bigcirc = 4$
$\triangle \div \bigcirc = \square$
$\square + \bigcirc = 5$

7
$\triangle + \square = 13$
$\triangle - \square = 5$
$\square + \bigcirc = 10$
$\bigcirc - \square = 2$

8
$\bigcirc + \square = 13$
$\square + 1 = \bigcirc$
$\triangle + \triangle = \square$
$\bigcirc + \triangle = 10$

9
$\square + \bigcirc = 15$
$\square - \bigcirc = 3$
$\triangle + \triangle = \bigcirc$
$\triangle + \triangle + \triangle = \square$

10
$\triangle + \bigcirc = 12$
$\triangle - \bigcirc = \square$
$\square + \square + 1 = \bigcirc$
$\square + \square + \square + 1 = 7$

Fraction fun

In these puzzles, some of the digits or fractions have been blotted out.
Find the missing numbers.

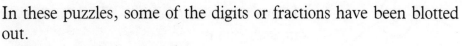

1 $\frac{1}{2} \times \Box = 5$

2 $\Box \times 8 = 4$

3 $\frac{1}{4} \times \Box = 3$

4 $\frac{1}{4} \times \Box = 6$

5 $\Box \times 18 = 9$

6 $\Box \times 24 = 12$

7 $\Box \times 24 = 6$

8 $\Box \times 12 = 3$

9 $\frac{1}{10} \times \Box = 3$

10 $\Box \times 40 = 4$

11 $\Box \times 40 = 10$

12 $\Box \times 40 = 20$

13 $\Box \times 40 = 8$

14 $\frac{1}{5} \times \Box = 8$

15 $\frac{1}{5} \times \Box = 10$

16 $\Box \times 22 = 11$

17 $\frac{1}{3} \times \Box = 9$

18 $\frac{1}{4} \times \Box = 4$

19 $\frac{1}{5} \times \Box = 4$

20 $\frac{1}{10} \times \Box = 9$

21 $\Box \times 18 = 6$

22 $\Box \times 60 = 30$

23 $\frac{1}{4} \times \Box = 8$

24 $\Box \times 15 = 3$

25 $\Box \times 15 = 5$

26 $\Box \times 25 = 5$

27 $\Box \times 30 = 3$

28 $\Box \times 30 = 5$

29 $\frac{1}{5} \times \Box = 6$

30 $\frac{1}{8} \times \Box = 3$

Coin puzzles

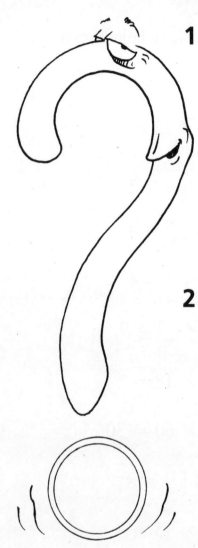

1 I have two piles of coins. Work out how many coins there are in each pile if:
  (a) the first pile has 7 more than the second and there are 47 coins altogether;
  (b) the first pile has 8 more than the second and there are 34 coins altogether;
  (c) the first pile has 7 fewer than the second and there are 23 coins altogether;
  (d) the first pile has 3 times as many as the second and there are 48 coins altogether;
  (e) the first pile has 4 times as many as the second and there are 30 coins altogether.

2 I have three piles of coins. Calculate how many coins there are in each pile if:
  (a) the second pile has 3 more than the first, the third has 3 more than the second and there are 27 coins altogether;
  (b) the first pile has 9 more than the second, the third has 1 less than the second and there are 41 coins altogether;
  (c) the second pile has twice as many as the first, the third has twice as many as the second and there are 56 coins altogether;
  (d) the second pile has twice as many as the first, the third has half as many as the first and there are 21 coins altogether;
  (e) the second pile has twice as many as the first, the third has twice as many as the second and the third has 9 more than the first;
  (f) the first pile has 3 times as many as the third, the second has 3 more than the third and there are 38 coins altogether.

© Mathematics Enrichment Book C Simon & Schuster Education 1993

Problems on a dartboard

1 In one game of darts, 3 and 5 are the only possible scores in one throw.
  (a) What scores are possible?
  (b) What scores are impossible?

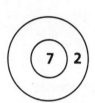

2 In another game of darts, 2 and 7 are the only possible values for a throw.
  (a) What scores are possible?
  (b) What scores are impossible?

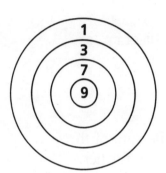

3 Robert threw four darts at this dartboard and all four hit a target.
  Which of the following numbers could his total score have been?

17, 22, 25, 18, 24, 11, 16, 31
What other totals could he have got?

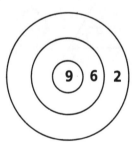

4 In a game of darts in which 9, 6 and 2 are the only possible scores, calculate:
  (a) the smallest number of throws needed to score exactly 34;
  (b) the greatest number of throws needed to score exactly 34.

Goldbach's conjectures

Goldbach's first conjecture was that 'every even number greater than 4 is the sum of two prime numbers'; for example:

14 = 3 + 11 or 14 = 7 + 7

1 Express the following even numbers as sums of two prime numbers.

(a) 16	**(c)** 46	**(e)** 92	**(g)** 38
(b) 24	**(d)** 84	**(f)** 72	**(h)** 98

Goldbach's second conjecture is that 'every odd number greater than 7 is the sum of three prime numbers'; for example:

13 = 5 + 5 + 3 or 13 = 3 + 3 + 7

and for fun we can write the second of these as a diagram, as shown at left.

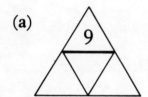

2 Express each number in these diagrams as the sum of three prime numbers. Under each diagram, write any further solutions you can find.

(a)   **(b)** 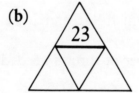 **(c)** 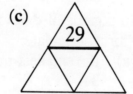 **(d)**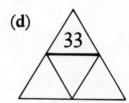

(e) 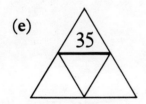 **(f)** 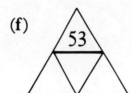 **(g)** 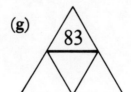 **(h)**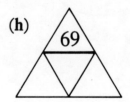

3 Test Goldbach's conjectures with other numbers. Do you think the conjectures are true?

© Mathematics Enrichment Book C Simon & Schuster Education 1993

Domino puzzles

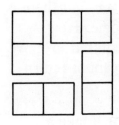

For these problems, you should use the grid paper with blank domino shapes, on page 88.

1 Arrange the four dominoes in each exercise in a hollow square (as shown at left) so that every side is equal to the number given below them.

(a)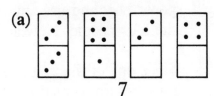
7

(b)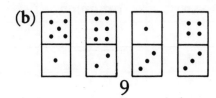
9

(c)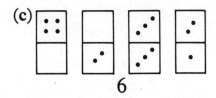
6

(d)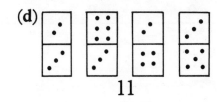
11

(e)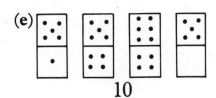
10

2 Arrange these dominoes in hollow squares so that in each exercise all sides equal the same sum.

(a)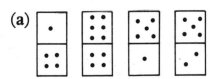

(b)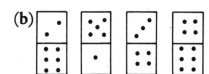

(c)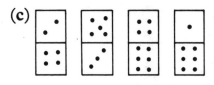

(d)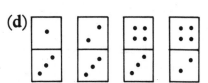

(e)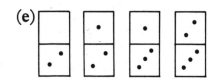

Boat trips

Four friends go on a picnic. They have to cross a river, but there is only one boat for hire and it can hold only three people. How many trips back and forth across the river will be required to move the four to the other side? Remember that the boat cannot return on its own.

Waiting to cross	Crossing or returning	After crossing
4	0	0
1	3 →	0
1	← 1	2
0	2 →	2
0	0	4

Draw up a table, as shown. Make a paper boat and use any models to represent the four people. Now act out the problem.

Since one of the first three people to cross must return to pick up the fourth person, if you start with four people, you will have three trips.

1 Complete this table for a boat that can hold only 3 people.

Number of people	Number of trips
1	1
2	1
3	1
4	3
5	
6	
7	
8	
9	
10	
11	
12	

2 Study your table carefully, then write down the number of trips required if:
   (a) 20 people go on a picnic;
   (b) 22 people go on a picnic.

3 What patterns have you noticed? Explain.

© Mathematics Enrichment Book C Simon & Schuster Education 1993

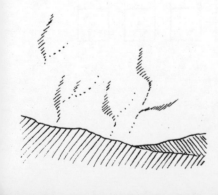

Cake-cutting time

For Jeremy's birthday, his dad made a birthday cake after dinner.

However, first his dad asked Jeremy to make eight round, flat 'cakes' out of modelling clay. Then he asked him to tackle the following challenges, in which he was to divide each cake into a given number of pieces with a given number of cuts, using a fairly blunt knife and straight-line cuts only.

If you cannot use modelling clay, use paper on which blank circles are drawn.

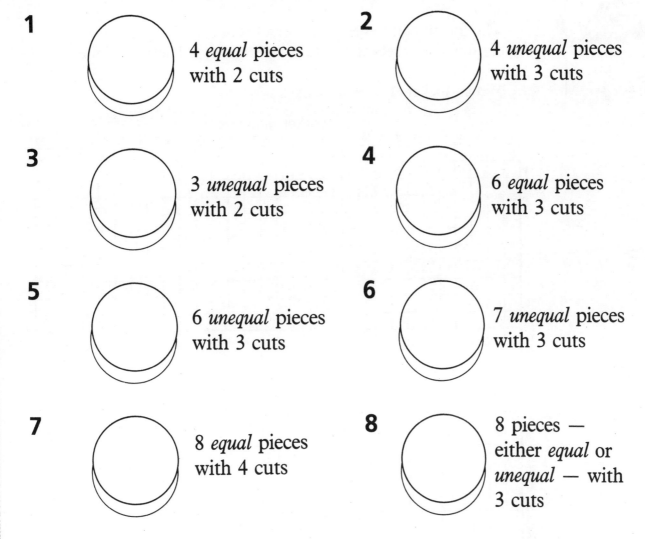

1 4 *equal* pieces with 2 cuts

2 4 *unequal* pieces with 3 cuts

3 3 *unequal* pieces with 2 cuts

4 6 *equal* pieces with 3 cuts

5 6 *unequal* pieces with 3 cuts

6 7 *unequal* pieces with 3 cuts

7 8 *equal* pieces with 4 cuts

8 8 pieces — either *equal* or *unequal* — with 3 cuts

Jeremy's dad promised that if Jeremy mastered the first seven challenges correctly, he would bake a cake for him the next day.

If Jeremy got the last one correct as well, his dad would bake him a cake every day for a week.

Would you have got seven cakes?

The locker problem

In a certain classroom there are 30 lockers numbered 1 to 30. There are also 30 children in the classroom.

One morning, the first child to arrive opens every locker.

The second child to arrive closes all the even-numbered lockers (2, 4, 6 → 30).

The third child goes to the lockers that are multiples of 3 — that is, lockers numbered 3, 6, 9 → 30; of these, this child opens the lockers that are closed, and closes the lockers that are open.

The fourth child goes to lockers 4, 8, 12 → 28 and does the same thing (reverses the state of the lockers). The rest of the 30 children continue this process.

Which lockers are eventually left open?

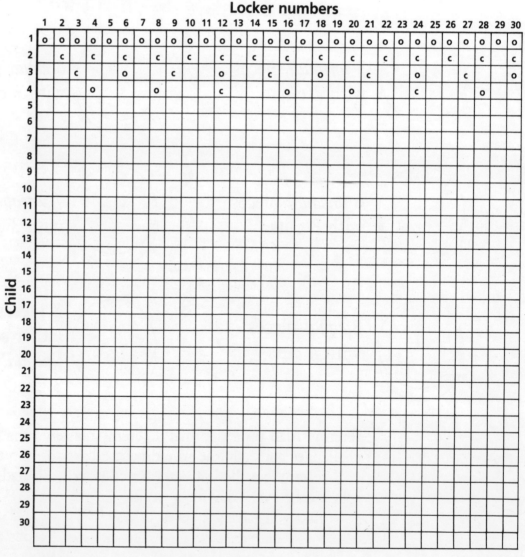

Locker numbers

Child	1	2	3	4	5	6	7	8	9	10	11	12	13	14	15	16	17	18	19	20	21	22	23	24	25	26	27	28	29	30
1	o	o	o	o	o	o	o	o	o	o	o	o	o	o	o	o	o	o	o	o	o	o	o	o	o	o	o	o	o	o
2		c		c		c		c		c		c		c		c		c		c		c		c		c		c		c
3			c			o			c			o			c			o			c			o			c			o
4				o				o				c				o				o				c				o		
5																														
6																														
7																														
8																														
9																														
10																														
11																														
12																														
13																														
14																														
15																														
16																														
17																														
18																														
19																														
20																														
21																														
22																														
23																														
24																														
25																														
26																														
27																														
28																														
29																														
30																														

Find the correct position

1 Guess the cards.

Four cards

lie face down on the table: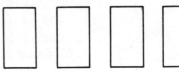

The cards are not in the order given above, but the following facts are known about them:

(a) The card with ★ is to the left of the card with △.

(b) The card with ◯ is not on the edge, and is to the right of the ★.

(c) The card with △ is between the card with ● and the card with ◯.

What is the order of the cards?

2 Here are four views of one cube.

(a) What are the shapes on the faces adjacent to (next to) ☐?
Now work out which shape is on the face opposite ☐.

(b) What are the shapes on the faces adjacent to ⊙? What shape is on the face opposite ⊙?

(c) What shape is on the face opposite ◖?

Problem solving: Using tables 2

To answer these questions, you could draw up tables and use guess-and-check.

I DO ALL MY PROBLEM SOLVING USING A TABLE.

1 Michelle and her younger sister, Mia, bought their mother a bracelet for her birthday.

If Michelle decided to contribute twice as much as Mia and the bracelet cost £24, how much did each girl pay?

Michelle's contribution	Mia's contribution	Total cost

2 The sum of the ages of three children is 35. The oldest, Imran, is twice the age of the youngest, Bruce. Gordon is 3 years older than Bruce.

How old is Imran?

Imran	Gordon	Bruce	Sum of their ages

3 The sum of the ages of three sisters — Monique, Laura and Amy — is 25. Monique is the oldest. Amy is 7 years younger than Monique. Laura is 3 years older than Amy.

What are the ages of the three girls?

Monique	Laura	Amy	Sum of their ages

4 Lemon drops come in packages of 3 for 20p. Chocolate mints cost 5p each. Tom bought 20 sweets and spent £1.20.

How many of each kind did he buy?

Lemon drops (20p a pkt)	Chocolate mints (5p each)	Total spent

5 Raspberries cost £3 for 1 kg and grapes cost £4 for 1 kg.

How many kilograms of each did Mrs Morgan buy if:
(a) she spent £18 and had 5 kg of fruit?
(b) she spent £12? Is there only one answer to this?

Raspberries	Grapes	Cost

The four 5's challenge

Insert mathematical signs in the groups of 5's to make each set a true number sentence.

Here is an example: 5   5   5   5 = 1 can be written as:

$(5 + 5 - 5) \div 5 = 1$ or $(5 \div .5) \div (5 \div .5) = 1$

Remember these points:

(a) $\sqrt{5 \times 5} = 5$
(b) $5! = 5 \times 4 \times 3 \times 2 \times 1$
(c) The number 55 may be used.
(d) $5 \div 0.5 = 10$ because there are 10 lots of 0.5 in 5.
(e) The statement $(5 + 5 - 5) \div 5 = 1$ is not considered to be different from $(5 - 5 + 5) \div 5 = 1$.
(f) Do not forget your order of operations:
     Brackets first.
     Multiplication and division next.
     Addition and subtraction last.
(g) Try to find find several solutions for most of the questions.

1	5 5 5 5 = 0		**12**	5 5 5 5 = 26
2	5 5 5 5 = 1		**13**	5 5 5 5 = 30
3	5 5 5 5 = 2		**14**	5 5 5 5 = 45
4	5 5 5 5 = 3		**15**	5 5 5 5 = 50
5	5 5 5 5 = 4		**16**	5 5 5 5 = 55
6	5 5 5 5 = 5		**17**	5 5 5 5 = 75
7	5 5 5 5 = 6		**18**	5 5 5 5 = 100
8	5 5 5 5 = 10		**19**	5 5 5 5 = 120
9	5 5 5 5 = 15		**20**	5 5 5 5 = 125
10	5 5 5 5 = 24		**21**	5 5 5 5 = 130
11	5 5 5 5 = 25		**22**	5 5 5 5 = 150

Make up some of your own.

Stars and shapes

1 Figures are *congruent* if they have the same size and shape.
Here are three examples of one shape. Can you divide each
one into the number of congruent shapes indicated above it?

(a) 2 congruent shapes   **(b)** 3 congruent shapes   **(c)** 4 congruent shapes

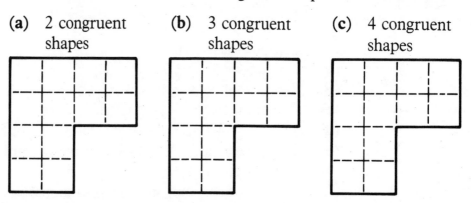

2 Use dot-squared paper (page 90) to do this exercise.
Three stars have been placed on a 9-dot square grid so that
there is only one star in any row or column.

(a) Place 4 stars on a 16-dot square grid so that there is only
one star in any row or column. How many different
solutions can you find?

(b) Place 4 stars on this 16-dot square grid so that there is no
more than one star along any of the lines drawn
(including all diagonals).

3 Place only 10 stars in the small squares of this figure in
such a way that there is an even number of stars in every row,
in every column and in the two diagonals. Use squared paper.

NOW GO ON TO BOOK D!

60

© Mathematics Enrichment Book C Simon & Schuster Education 1993

Solutions Book C

What's the value? (page 1)

This is a very difficult challenge, especially since the way to discover the value of each shape cannot be found by taking the equations in order. Children have to work out where to start and how to proceed from the known to the unknown. However, they usually enjoy the puzzle and get a real sense of achievement when they complete it.

Lines 4 and 5 are both good starts, since $1 \times 1 = 1$, so ▯ = 1, and $2 + 2 = 2 \times 2$, so ▮ = 2.
Line 3 confirms these two values, as $1 + 1 = 2$.
Line 7 now tells us that $4 \div 2 = 2$, so we know that ☐ = 4.
Continuing:
Line 8 is now $4 + 1 = $ ▣, so ▣ = 5.
Line 10 is ⊠ $- 4 = 5$, so ⊠ = 9.
Line 11 is $5 + 2 = $ ◹, so ◹ = 7.
Line 1 is $7 + 1 = $ ⊠, so ⊠ = 8.
Line 6 is $9 \div$ ⊞ $= $ ⊞, so ⊞ = 3.
Line 2 is $2 \times 3 = $ ▨, so ▨ = 6.
The last few lines need not be done in this order.

Rolling boxes (page 2)

Children are not expected to visualise the position of the symbols as the boxes are rolled. They should carry out the experiments.

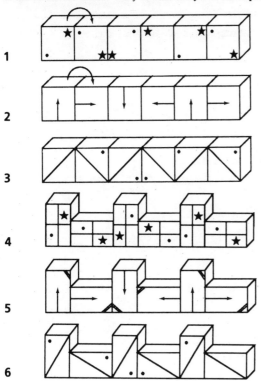

Find my rule (page 3)

	Rule	Missing numbers		Rule	Missing numbers
1	×4, +7	12, 19	6	×9, −5	45, 40
2	−7, ×6	3, 18	7	−4, ×7	2, 14
3	−3, ×9	6, 54	8	÷3, ×8	2, 16
4	÷2, + 5	3, 8	9	÷4, ×5	4, 20
5	×8, −11	48, 37	10	×6, ÷2	6; 48, 24

Making up their own rules allows children to be creative and may stretch them further. They may find that the operations and numbers need to be chosen with care if they wish to avoid using decimals or negative members.

Digits and numbers (page 4)

1 9995		**6** 9876		**11** 9990	
2 1005		**7** 9872		**12** 10 000	
3 1000		**8** 532		**13** 11 111	
4 99 999		**9** 235		**14** 88 888	
5 1023		**10** 1011		**15** 9870	

Picture graphs (page 5)

1 (a) 18 (6 × 3)   (e) pies; 3 (1 × 3)
   (b) 15 (5 × 3)   (f) 84 (28 × 3)
   (c) 12 (4 × 3)   (g) 6 sandwiches were sold;
   (d) chips; 21 (7 × 3)   ∴ 9 were left.

2 Note that since ◖ = 4 balls, ◖ = 2 balls.
   (a) (i) 24 (6 × 4) (iii) 6 (1½ × 4)
      (ii) 8 (2 × 4) (iv) 18 (4½ × 4)
   (b) 72

3 This provides children with an opportunity to pose their own questions. This is a vital and often neglected part of the data handling process.

Problem solving: guess and check (page 6)

1 Using the numbers 1, 2, 3, 4, 5, 6 and 7, we need to find three number pairs that have the same sum.
   (a) If 1 is in the centre : ① 2 3 4 5 6 7, the linked pairs each add to 9, so the sum along each line is 10.
   (b) If 4 is in the centre: 1 2 3 ④ 5 6 7, the linked pairs each add to 8, so the sum along each line is 12.
   (c) If 7 is in the centre: 1 2 3 4 5 6 ⑦, the linked pairs each add to 7, so the sum along each line is 14.

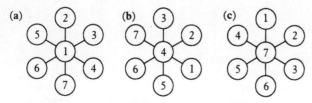

The position of the numbers in the outer circles may vary as long as the pairs are the same as those indicated above.

2 In (a), (b) and (c) the number circled is in the centre of the figure. The number pairs are linked and can be placed on opposite arms of the figure.

(a) ① 2 3 4 5 6 7 8 9   (line total: 12)

(b) 1 2 3 4 ⑤ 6 7 8 9   (line total: 15)

(c) 1 2 3 4 5 6 7 8 ⑨   (line total: 18)

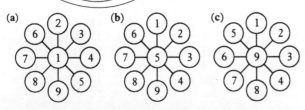

Remember that there are many other possible solutions.

3 The only possible line totals are those given. Children should be encouraged to explain their answer. The solutions for 1 and 2 above suggest why this is so.

Problem solving: Working systematically 1 (page 7)

1

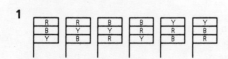

2 Altogether there are 27 possible colour combinations. Given here are the remaining 25.

Children should be encouraged to work them out systematically — without some guidance and discussion, it is doubtful whether they would find most of the possibilities.

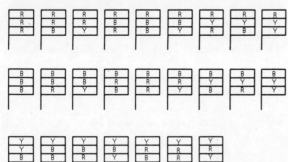

3

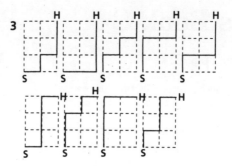

4 There are only two other possible patterns.

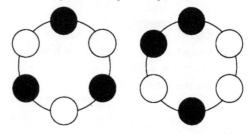

How many? (page 8)

In questions 1, 3 and 5, working systematically and counting all the different sized shapes is essential. Some children may decide to set out work in a table for clarity and organisation.

Provide the children with copies of the figures on pages 87 and 88, since they may need to shade the shapes as they count them, as shown in these middle-sized examples from question 1:

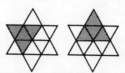

1 20 triangles: 12 single, 6 middle-sized, 2 large.

2 (a)   6 lines   **(b)**   10 lines

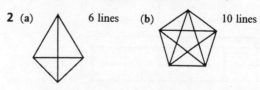

3 18 parallelograms: 6 small, 7 double (illustrated below), 2 treble, 2 quadruple, 1 large.

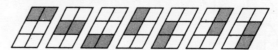

4 10 segments: XY, XZ, XU, XW, YZ, YU, YW, ZU, ZW, UW

5 18 squares: 8 single, 5 (2 × 2), 4 (3 × 3), 1 (4 × 4)

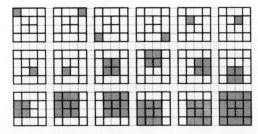

What is my message? (page 9)

The order of the problems is not necessarily that in which, as clues, the children will have to use them. Some children may in fact guess the messages and so skip some of the mathematics. .

1
$$\underset{1\ 8\ 3\ 5}{\text{R O C K'N}}\ \ \underset{1\ 8\ 2\ 2}{\text{R O L L}}\ \ \underset{4\ 0}{\text{I S}}\ \ \underset{6\ 9\ 7}{\text{F U N}}$$

$2 \times 2 = 2 + 2$	$3 + 2 = 5$	$5 \div 5 = 1$
$1 \times 1 = 1$	$3^2 = 9$	$2 \times 0 = 0$
$1 + 1 = 2$	$2^2 = 4$	$7 \times 5 = 35$
$3 - 2 = 1$	$2 \times 4 = 8$	$49 \div 7 = 7$
$3 \times 2 = 6$	$6 - 6 = 0$	

Code: $\dfrac{R}{1}\ \dfrac{L}{2}\ \dfrac{C}{3}\ \dfrac{I}{4}\ \dfrac{K}{5}\ \dfrac{F}{6}\ \dfrac{N}{7}\ \dfrac{O}{8}\ \dfrac{U}{9}\ \dfrac{S}{0}$

2
$$\underset{4\ 9\ 1\ 8\ 7}{\text{M A T H S}}\ \ \underset{3\ 7}{\text{I S}}\ \ \underset{6\ 2\ 5\ 5\ 6}{\text{Y U K K Y}}$$

$\begin{array}{r}1837\\ +\ 37\\ \hline 1874\end{array}$	$\begin{array}{r}94\\ 94\\ +\ 94\\ \hline 282\end{array}$	
$4 \div 4 = 1$	$6 \times 6 = 36$	
$1 \times 1 = 1$	$1 + 2 = 3$	
$3^2 = 9$	$9 - 5 = 4$	
$2^2 = 4$	$45 \div 5 = 9$	
$5 \times 5 = 25$	$32 \div 8 = 4$	

Code: $\dfrac{T}{1}\ \dfrac{U}{2}\ \dfrac{I}{3}\ \dfrac{M}{4}\ \dfrac{K}{5}\ \dfrac{Y}{6}\ \dfrac{S}{7}\ \dfrac{H}{8}\ \dfrac{A}{9}$

Multiplication table squares (page 10)

This is an exciting way to test and reinforce multiplication tables. Children can also make up other exercises and test each other.

1

X	3	5	4	7
2	6	10	8	14
8	24	40	32	56
3	9	15	12	21
9	27	45	36	63

2

X	4	6	2	7
5	20	30	10	35
3	12	18	6	21
8	32	48	16	56
6	24	36	12	42

The missing horizontal number is 2, since $5 \times 2 = 10$. The missing vertical numbers are 3 and 8, since $3 \times 6 = 18$ and $4 \times 8 = 32$.

3

X	2	3	9	5
2	4	6	18	10
8	16	24	72	40
7	14	21	63	35
4	8	12	36	20

4

X	7	4	11	5
2	14	8	22	10
3	21	12	33	15
9	63	36	99	45
4	28	16	44	20

5

X	3	8	5	10
4	12	32	20	40
5	15	40	25	50
3	9	24	15	30
9	27	72	45	90

6

X	9	2	7	8
3	27	6	21	24
8	72	16	56	64
6	54	12	42	48
2	18	4	14	16

7

X	5	4	6	8
1	5	4	6.	8
6	30	24	36	48
9	45	36	54	72
4	20	16	24	32

8

X	5	2	10	8
5	25	10	50	40
8	40	16	80	64
3	15	6	30	24
10	50	30	100	80

How does it start? (page 11)

This can be made into a challenging game that children can have fun playing. One says: 'I think of a number, I add 3 to it, I multiply the result by 2 and my answer is 14. Find the number I first thought of'. The game can be played for hours, and children love it.

To find the number that belongs in the START circle of the example, begin with the end circle and work backwards, using the inverse of each given operation.

The inverse of add is subtract.
The inverse of subtract is add.
The inverse of multiply is divide.
The inverse of divide is multiply.

The reason for this is that if in the original flow chart the total of 14 was reached by multiplying a number by 2, to find that number by working backwards we must divide 14 by 2, so that the number must be 7. Similarly, if 7 was the result of adding 3 to a number, we find the number by subtracting 3 from 7.

1 ② ← | Subtract 4: $6 - 4 = 2$ | ← | Divide by 3: $18 \div 3 = 6$ | ← ⑱

2 ⑦ ← | Add 5: $2 + 5 = 7$ | ← | Divide by 3: $6 \div 3 = 2$ | ← ⑥

3 ⑤ ← | Subtract 7: $12 - 7 = 5$ | ← | Multiply by 2: $6 \times 2 = 12$ | ← ⑥

4 ⑤ ← | Subtract 3: $8 - 3 = 5$ | ← | Divide by 3: $24 \div 3 = 8$ | ← | Add 10: $14 + 10 = 24$ | ← ⑭

5 ④ ← | Find the square root of 16 (i.e. 4) or ask 'what number squared is 16?' | ← | Add 6: $10 + 6 = 16$ | ← | Multiply by 2: $5 \times 2 = 10$ | ← ⑤

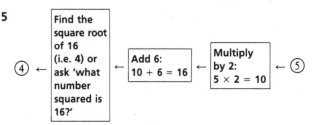

6 Whilst investigating using different end numbers, children will encounter numbers other than positive whole numbers. A calculator may be useful here.

Missing numbers (page 12)

	Number	Rule	Number	Rule	Number	Rule	Number	Rule	Number
1		+8		×2		−10		*÷2	
2		+8		×2		−10		÷2	
3	9		17		34		24		12
4	10		18		36		26		13
5	12		20		40		30		15
6	5		13		26		16		8
7	1		9		18		8		4
8	22		30		60		50		25
9	18		26		52		42		21
10	15		23		46		36		18
11	17		25		50		40		20
12	29		37		74		64		32

* Divide by 2 *or* subtract half.

In exercises 1 and 2, children need to find the rule for each shape. In numbers 3, 4 and 5 they are expected to apply the rule, starting with the first given number. In nos 6–12 they should work backwards as well.

For example, in number 12: 32 was reached by dividing a number by 2, so to find that number by working backwards we must multiply 32 by 2, making the number 64. Again working backwards: 64 was reached by subtracting 10 from a number; to find it we need to add 10 to 64, giving us 74.

Complete the exercise in the same way.

Number squares 1 (page 13)

Guess-and-check will be a very useful strategy here. Suggested starting points are given for exercises 2–5.

1

5	3	4	12
2	4	5	11
1	5	2	8
8	12	11	

A = 3
B = 1
C = 4
D = 5
E = 2

In the second row and the third column C + D = 9, therefore A = 3 (in the first row). Now use trial and error to find the value of C and D: if D = 4 and C = 5, then B = 2, which is impossible, since we know that E = 2. Therefore, D = 5 and C = 4. Alternatively, we could work from the bottom row, where B + D = 6, and then use trial and error.

2

3	1	2	6
4	5	2	11
1	3	4	8
8	9	8	

A = 1
B = 4
C = 5
D = 3
E = 2

Start: C + D = 8 *or* E + D = 5

4

5	1	3	9
4	2	6	12
3	4	2	9
12	7	11	

A = 5
B = 2
C = 6
D = 1
E = 3
F = 4

Start: F + E = 7 *or* D + E = 4

3

4	5	3	12
2	3	1	6
1	4	2	7
7	12	6	

A = 3
B = 5
*C = 1 or 2
*D = 2 or 1
E = 4

*These values can be transposed.

Start: D + C = 3 *or* E + B = 9

5

6	1	3	10
3	2	4	9
2	3	5	10
11	6	12	

A = 3
B = 2
C = 1
D = 6
E = 4
F = 5

Start: B + A = 5 *or* A + F = 8

Investigating magic squares (page 14)

1 Yes; the sum is 21.
2 Yes; the sum is 45.

3 (a) The sum is 12.   (b) The sum is 30.

16	2	12
6	10	14
8	18	4

(c) The sums are 45, 75 and 150 respectively.

(d) The sum is $7\frac{1}{2}$.

4	$\frac{1}{2}$	3
$\frac{3}{2}$	$\frac{5}{2}$	$\frac{7}{2}$
2	$\frac{9}{2}$	1

(e) The sums are $16\frac{1}{2}$ (for $+\frac{1}{2}$) and $13\frac{1}{2}$ (for $-\frac{1}{2}$). In each case the square is still magic.

4 Yes.

Completing the lines (page 15)

1 Note that in the shaded lines of each square all the numbers were given, thus providing the magic sums. In (a) and (b), the numbers that should be looked for first are indicated with arrows.

(a) Magic sum: 34

→7	6	11	10
14	9	8	3
12	15	2	5
1	4	13	16

(b) Magic sum: 34

8	11	2	13
10	5	16	3
15	4	9	6
1	14	7	12

(c) Magic sum: 42

8	15	14	5
9	11	18	4
12	6	7	17
13	10	3	16

(d) Magic sum: 72

33	5	7	27
11	23	21	17
19	15	13	25
9	29	31	3

(e) Magic sum: 62

23	9	10	20
12	18	17	15
16	14	13	19
11	21	22	8

2 (a)

1	3	5	2	4
5	2	4	1	3
4	1	3	5	2
3	5	2	4	1
2	4	1	3	5

(b)

1	2	3	4	5
3	4	5	1	2
5	1	2	3	4
2	3	4	5	1
4	5	1	2	3

Largest and smallest (page 16)

1 (a) $9 + 8 = 17$
(b) $9 + 8 + 7 = 24$
(c) $9 + 8 + 7 + 6 = 30$
(d) $9 - 1 = 8$
(e) $9 + 8 - 1 = 16$
(f) $9 - 2 - 1 = 6$
(g) 98
(h) $98 + 7 = 105$
(i) $98 - 1 = 97$
(j) $97 + 86 = 183$
(k) $98 - 12 = 86$
(l) $98 - 12 - 3 = 83$

2 (a) $1 + 2 = 3$
(b) $1 + 2 + 3 = 6$
(c) $1 + 2 + 3 + 4 = 10$
(d) $2 - 1 = 1$
or
$3 - 2$
$4 - 3$
$5 - 4$
$6 - 5$
$7 - 6$
$8 - 7$
$9 - 8$
(e) $2 + 1 - 3 = 0$
or
$3 + 1 - 4$
$3 + 2 - 5$
$4 + 1 - 5$
$4 + 2 - 6$
$4 + 3 - 7$
$5 + 1 - 6$
$5 + 2 - 7$
$5 + 3 - 8$
$5 + 4 - 9$
$6 + 1 - 7$
$6 + 2 - 8$
$6 + 3 - 9$
$7 + 1 - 8$
$7 + 2 - 9$
$8 + 1 - 9$
(f) $3 - 1 - 2 = 0$
or
$4 - 1 - 3$
$5 - 2 - 3$
$6 - 1 - 5$
$6 - 2 - 4$
$7 - 1 - 6$
$7 - 2 - 5$
$7 - 3 - 4$
$8 - 1 - 7$
$8 - 2 - 6$
$8 - 3 - 5$
$9 - 1 - 8$
$9 - 2 - 7$
$9 - 3 - 6$
$9 - 4 - 5$
(g) 12
(h) $12 + 3 = 15$
or
$13 + 2$
(i) $12 - 9 = 3$
(j) $13 + 24 = 37$
or
$14 + 23$
(k) $21 - 19 = 2$
or
$31 - 29$
$41 - 39$
$51 - 49$
$61 - 59$
$71 - 69$
$81 - 79$
(l) $41 - 39 - 2 = 0$
or
$51 - 49 - 2$
$61 - 59 - 2$
$71 - 69 - 2$
$81 - 79 - 2$
or
$51 - 48 - 3$
$51 - 43 - 8$
$51 - 42 - 9$
$61 - 58 - 3$
$61 - 57 - 4$
$61 - 54 - 7$
$61 - 53 - 8$
$61 - 52 - 9$
$71 - 68 - 3$
$71 - 67 - 4$
$71 - 63 - 8$
$71 - 62 - 9$
$81 - 76 - 5$
$81 - 75 - 6$
$81 - 72 - 9$
or
$45 - 39 - 6$
$46 - 39 - 7$
and so on

Multiplying puzzles (page 17)

Children should be encouraged to use calculators to do these puzzles.

1 (a) $32 \times 4 = 128$ (b) $41 \times 32 = 1312$ Children should realise that 4 and 3 must be tens, not units, in order to get the largest product.

2 (a) $87 \times 9 = 783$ (b) $74 \times 92 = 6808$ (c) $874 \times 9 = 7866$

3 (a) $27 \times 8 = 216$ or $24 \times 9 = 216$ or $72 \times 3 = 216$

Note that in these solutions the digits are not different: $54 \times 4 = 216$ $36 \times 6 = 216$

To find all possible solutions, children could write down all the one-digit factors of 216: 2, 3, 4, 6, 8, 9. Now consider all possible combinations of each factor with two other digits to make the given product.

(b) $56 \times 2 = 112$ or $28 \times 4 = 112$ or $14 \times 8 = 112$ or $16 \times 7 = 112$

Counting cubes (page 18)

Most children will find it necessary to build the towers in order to count the cubes in each layer, and can use the cubes to check their answers. They should be encouraged to look for patterns.

1 (a)

top	1
2nd	3
Total	4

(b)

top	1
2nd	3
3rd	6
Total	10

(c)

top	1
2nd	3
3rd	6
4th	10
Total	20

2 (a)

top	2
2nd	6
Total	8

(b)

top	2
2nd	6
3rd	12
Total	20

(c)

top	2
2nd	6
3rd	12
4th	20
Total	40

3 (a)

top	4
Total	4

(b)

top	4
2nd	16
Total	20

(c)

top	4
2nd	16
3rd	36
Total	56

4 (a)

top	1
2nd	9
Total	10

(b)

top	1
2nd	9
3rd	25
Total	35

(c)

top	1
2nd	9
3rd	25
4th	49
Total	84

Halves and quarters (page 19)

In this investigation there are many different shapes to be made; given here are some possible examples. Children should be encouraged to work systematically, using copies of the squared paper on page 83.

Check that all versions are in fact different — that is, no 'new' shape is simply an existing one presented in a different position. There should be a thorough discussion with children of which figures (if any) are the same, and why.

1 (a)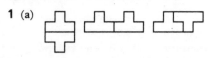

(b)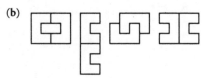

(c)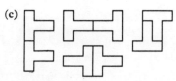

2 Example shape

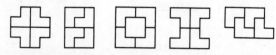

(a)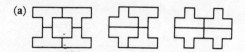

(b)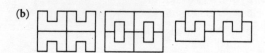

(c)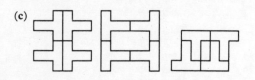

Puzzles with shapes (page 20)

1

 triangle and   square

2 (a)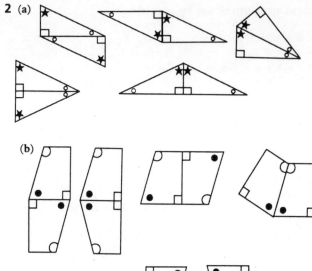

(b)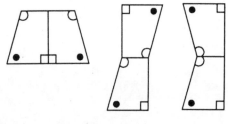

How many routes? (page 21)

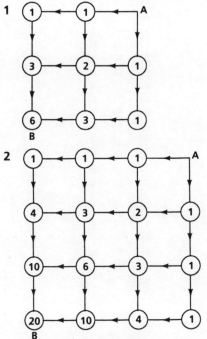

Figure 1 is embodied in figure 2.

For each point that has one arrow pointing to it along adjacent arms, there is only one route.

For each point that has two arrows pointing to it ($\downarrow \leftarrow$), the number of routes is the sum of the numbers on the two arms.

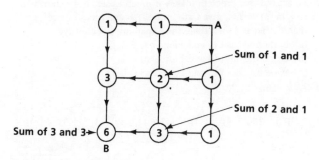

Polyiamonds (page 22)

For these exercises, children should be provided with isometric grid paper on page 86.

1 4 pentiamonds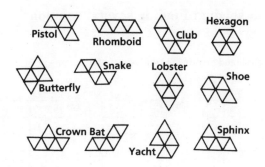

2 12 hexiamonds
Their names were given by T. H. O'Beirne, the Glasgow mathematician who invented the name 'polyiamonds' in 1965.

Pistol Rhomboid Club Hexagon
Snake Lobster Shoe Butterfly
Crown Bat Yacht Sphinx

Strange maths symbols 1 (page 23)

Children might find it useful to repeat orally the meaning of the relevant symbol as they find the value of each expression.

1 (a) $6 + 3 = 9$ (d) $20 + 4 = 24$
  (b) $10 + 4 = 14$ (e) $16 + 5 = 21$
  (c) $8 + 2 = 10$ (f) $20 + 5 = 25$

2 (a) $9 - 6 = 3$ (d) $100 - 8 = 92$
  (b) $25 - 8 = 17$ (e) $64 - 10 = 54$
  (c) $16 - 4 = 12$ (f) $1 - 16 = -15$

3 (a) $10 \div 2 = 5$ (d) $20 \div 2 = 10$
  (b) $10 \div 2 = 5$ (e) $28 \div 2 = 14$
  (c) $20 \div 2 = 10$ (f) $28 \div 2 = 14$

The symbol $\star$ will only produce a whole number if the second number is even. The # needs to have two odds or two even numbers if the result is to be a whole number.

Letter values (page 24)

1 B = 5

$$\begin{array}{r} 51 \\ \times\ 5 \\ \hline 255 \end{array}$$

2 C = 6

$$\begin{array}{r} 61 \\ \times\ 6 \\ \hline 366 \end{array}$$

3 A = 6

$$\begin{array}{r} 46 \\ \times\ 6 \\ \hline 276 \end{array}$$

4 M = 2
N = 3

$$\begin{array}{r} 23 \\ \times\ 3 \\ \hline 69 \end{array}$$

5 U = 2
V = 4
W = 7

$$\begin{array}{r} 247 \\ \times\ 6 \\ \hline 1482 \end{array}$$

6 Since RR must equal 11 (as P + Q must be less than 22), the possible solutions are

$$\begin{array}{r} 9 \\ +\ 2 \\ \hline 11 \end{array} \quad \begin{array}{r} 8 \\ +\ 3 \\ \hline 11 \end{array} \quad \begin{array}{r} 7 \\ +\ 4 \\ \hline 11 \end{array}$$

$$\begin{array}{r} 6 \\ +\ 5 \\ \hline 11 \end{array} \quad \text{and} \quad \begin{array}{r} 2 \\ +\ 9 \\ \hline 11 \end{array}$$

7 Since the units digit of D + E + F is F, the units digit of D + E is 0, so D + E = 10. Therefore, D = 1 and E = 9. F is any other one-digit number: 2, 3, 4, 5, 6, 7, 8 or 0.

8 J = 8
K = 9

$$\begin{array}{r} 89 \\ +\ 9 \\ \hline 98 \end{array}$$

9 G = 1
H = 0
L = 9

$$\begin{array}{r} 91 \\ +\ 9 \\ \hline 100 \end{array}$$

10 C must be an even number and C + C + C + C is less than 10, therefore C = 2.
    D = 3, as D + D + D + D ends in 2, and E = 9

$$\begin{array}{r} 23 \\ 23 \\ 23 \\ +\ 23 \\ \hline 92 \end{array}$$

11 Since the units digit of Y + W + X is Y, the units digit of W + X is O, therefore W + X = 10. From the second column, using a similar argument and carrying 1, 1 + W + Y = 10. Now W can only be 1 or 2, as the sum of the three two-digit numbers is less than 300. By trial and error it is then shown that W = 1, X = 9 and Y = 8.

12 S = 1
P = 3
Q = 4

$$\begin{array}{r} 34 \\ 34 \\ +\ 43 \\ \hline 111 \end{array}$$

13 W = 1
T = 0
V = 9

$$\begin{array}{r} 101 \\ -\ 91 \\ \hline 10 \end{array}$$

14 Only 3 × 5 ends in a 5; therefore N = 5, L = 1 and M = 8.

$$\begin{array}{r} 185 \\ 185 \\ +\ 185 \\ \hline 555 \end{array}$$

15 B = 1
A = 9
D = 0

$$\begin{array}{r} 991 \\ +\ 119 \\ \hline 1110 \end{array}$$

Problem solving: Working systematically 2 (page 25)

It is important in all these problems for children to find their own ways of recording.

1 (a) 3 presents   (b) 12 presents

2 20 presents

3 (a) 6 code words:
A B C
A C B
B A C
B C A
C A B
C B A

(b) 27: First start with A (illustrated), then with B and then with C.
A A A
A A B
A A C
A B A
A B B
A B C
A C A
A C B
A C C

4

1st	2nd	3rd
A	M	S
A	S	M
M	A	S
M	S	A
S	A	M
S	M	A

5 4 ways:

Bowl	Fish			
A	4	3	2	1
B	1	2	3	4

6

Shirts	Shorts	Jumpers
blue	navy	black
blue	white	black
blue	navy	red
blue	white	red
yellow	navy	black
yellow	white	black
yellow	navy	red
yellow	white	red

7 2 g
5 g
7 g
10 g
12 g
15 g
17 g

8 Giving the amounts all in pence 10, 20, 30, 40, 50, 60, 70, 80, 90, 100

Problem solving: Working backwards
(page 26)

To find all the solutions, we started with the final number and then worked backwards.

1 6: 9 multiplied by 2 gives 18, or 18 divided by 2 will give 9. Then 6 has to be added to 3 to give 9 or 3 must be subtracted from 9 to give 6. Now work through the problem to check the answer: $6 + 3 = 9$; $9 \times 2 = 18$.
2 5: 10 is doubled to give 20 and 5 is doubled to give 10.
3 12: 6 is added to 4 to give 10, and 12 is halved to give 6.
4 13: 6 is doubled to give 12, and 7 is subtracted from 13 to give 6.
5 10: 5 added to 9 gives 14, and 10 halved gives 5.
6 8: 4 doubled gives 8, and 8 halved gives 4.
7 6: Halving and then doubling or doubling and then halving will result in any number that you start with.
8 5 **9** 8 **10** 9 **11** 4 **12** 16 **13** 4 **14** 3 **15** 8
16 9 **17** 3 **18** 4
19 2: Before the result was halved, it was 6; before 2 was added it was 4, and before it was squared it was 2.

Problem solving: Act it out (page 27)

1 6 coins; given any coin, 6 others of the same value will fit around it exactly.
2 To act out this problem makes it much easier; if we start with £25, in (a) we first give Catherine £1, as she gets £1 more than Fiona, and then share the remaining £24 equally.
  (a) Catherine has £13 and Fiona has £12.
  (b) Catherine has £14 and Fiona has £11.
  (c) Catherine has £15 and Fiona has £10.
3 Total value: £1.77

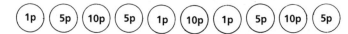

Problem solving: Finding several solutions
(page 28)

1 Children should be provided with squared paper or 4 × 4 grid paper on page 85.

* Note that square (g) is in fact the same as square (d), since each can be rotated to form the other. Discuss this with the children.

2 7 other possibilities

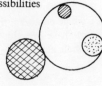 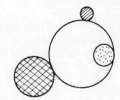

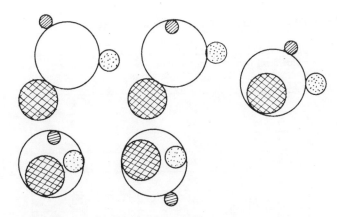

Working systematically is very helpful in this exercise. In the solutions given, the largest of the three was first drawn touching the outside while the smaller circles varied, and then the largest was drawn on the inside.

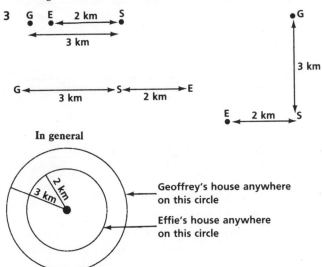

(Some very bright children will be capable of drawing this diagram.)

Problem solving: Using tables 1 (page 29)

1 Students can use guess-and-check, drawing up the table:

Esi	Marc	Total marbles
12	9	21

Alternatively, they can act out the problem. Start with 21 marbles or counters and give three to Esi, since she has three more than Marc.

Now the remaining 18 marbles can be divided equally between them; therefore Esi has 12 marbles (3 + 9) and Marc has 9 marbles.

2

Ice-creams (£1)	Ice-lollies (50p)	Total spent
6	8	£10

3

	5p coins	10p coins	Total coins	Total amount
(a)	4	2	6	40p
(b)	6	5	11	80p
(c)	3	3	6	45p
(d)	2	6	8	70p
(e)	6	2	8	50p

Problem solving: With extra information (page 30)

Children should discuss which information they did not use.

They could be asked to make up some problems that give unnecessary information, or even to create some that have insufficient information.

	Solutions	Extra information
1	Steve weighed 32 kg.	• Yoko weighed 9 kg more than Steve.
2	Kate Zara Lisa Layla 95 cm 90 cm 92 cm 98 cm	• Zara and Lisa are cousins. • Layla is 13 years old.
3	Kate Lisa Layla Zara 252 cm 255 cm 260 cm 265 cm	• Zara jumped 4 cm further than her best friend, Rhonda.
4	Marc Grandma Happy Mrs Happy Mr Happy Jenny	• Last night Jenny sat next to her brother and they had a fight. • Marc did not like the vegetable soup and his mother made him eat it. • Jenny loved the cake Grandma made.

Who am I? (page 31)

There are many different ways to solve these conundrums. One possible method is given here for numbers 3 to 14.

1 2
2 1
3 15: List the two-digit numbers less than 20: 10, 11, 12, 13, 14, 15, 16, 17, 18, 19. Now eliminate by crossing out all the numbers which are neither odd nor composite: ~~10, 11, 12, 13, 14~~, 15, ~~16, 17, 18, 19~~, and underline the odd composite number: <u>15</u>.
4 36: This is the only square number greater than 29 and less than 42.
   List the square numbers: 1, 4, 9, 16, 25, 36, 49, 64, and eliminate those less than 29 and those greater than 42.
5 13: List the primes and underline the sixth: 2, 3, 5, 7, 11, <u>13</u>.
6 30: List the two-digit numbers less than 40 and divisible by 10: 10, 20, 30. Now eliminate those not divisible by 3.

7 12: List the numbers divisible   by 4: 4, 8, <u>12</u>, 16
                                        and 3: 3, 6, 9, <u>12</u>
                                        and 2: 2, 4, 6, 8, 10, <u>12</u>
until one number occurs in all three cases.

8 25: List the two-digit square numbers: 16, 25, 36, 49, 64, 81; circle ⑯ and ㉕ , in which the sum of the digits is 7, and underline the one that is divisible by 5: <u>25</u>.

9 24: List the even numbers greater than 20 and less than 30: 22, 24, 26, 28. Now underline the number that is divisible by 3: <u>24</u>.

10 18: List the even two-digit numbers less than 25: 12, 14, 16, 18, 20, 22, 24. Now underline the number the sum of whose digits is 9: <u>18</u>. Check that this number is divisible by 3.

11 60: List two-digit numbers greater than 45 and less than 90 that are divisible by 10: 50, 60, 70, 80; underline the number is divisible by 3: <u>60</u>.

12 30: List the two-digit numbers the sum of whose digits is 3: 12, 21, 30. Now underline the number that is divisible by 5 and 2: <u>30</u>.

13 14: List the two-digit numbers less than 25 that are divisible by 7: 14, 21. Now underline the number that is also divisible by 2: <u>14</u>.

14 24: List the two-digit numbers less than 30 that are divisible by 8: 16, 24. Now underline the number that is also divisible by 6: <u>24</u>.

Perimeter and area investigation (page 32)

Children should be provided with either a geoboard or dot paper (p. 89).

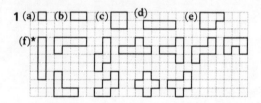

1 (a) (b) (c) (d) (e)
(f)*

* The figures in (f) are eleven of the twelve pentominoes. Figure (e) is the twelfth.

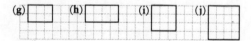

(g) (h) (i) (j)

2 It is not possible.

Growing squares and triangles (page 33)

1 (a)

Side (cm)	Perimeter (cm)	Area (sq. cm)
1	4	1
2	8	4
3	12	9
4	16	16
5	20	25
6	24	36
10	40	100
	The perimeter of each square is four times the length of a side.	The area of each square is the square of the length of a side.

(b) The perimeter and the area can in each case be predicted by following the patterns given in (a).

2 (a)

Side (units)	Perimeter (units)	Area (triang-grids)
1	3	1
2	6	4
3	9	9
4	12	16
5	15	25
6	18	36
10	30	100
	The perimeter of each equilateral triangle is three times the length of a side.	The area of each equilateral triangle (*measured in triangular grids*) is the square of the length of a side.

(b) The perimeters and areas can be predicted by following the patterns given in (a).

Perimeter puzzles (page 34)

Squared paper is essential for these exercises.

Children should check their figures to make sure they are all different — that no one figure is the same as another, but turned to a different position.

1 (a) 16 cm

(b)

2 (a) 14 cm

(b) 12 cm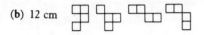

(c) 10 cm

(d) 8 cm

3 Since all four sides of a square are equal, each side is 9 cm. Numbers 4 and 5 can also be done using guess-and-check and drawing up a table.

4 From the diagram, the perimeter (60 m) has six equal sections; therefore one section is 10 m and the length is 20 m (2 × 10). If children have difficulty with this problem, solve a simpler one using a perimeter of 6 m and drawing the figure on squared paper.

5 This perimeter (48 m) has eight equal sections; therefore the width (one section) is 6 m and the length (three sections) is 18 m. Similarly, a simpler problem can be solved using a perimeter of 8 m and drawing the figure on squared paper:

```
      3 cm
1 cm ▭▭▭ 1 cm        Next use a perimeter
      3 cm            of 16 m:
```
```
        6 cm
2 cm ▭▭▭▭▭▭
```

6 The large table has 10 equal sections to total 20 m. Therefore the side of a square is 2 m and the perimeter of a square is 8 m.

Palindromic numbers (page 35)

1 (a)
```
   59
   95
  ───
  154
  451
  ───
  605
  506
 ────
 1111
 ────
```
(b)
```
   78
   87
  ───
  165
  561
  ───
  726
  627
 ────
 1353
 3531
 ────
 4884
 ────
```
(c)
```
   79
   97
  ───
  176
  671
  ───
  847
  748
 ────
 1595
 5951
 ────
 7546
 6457
 ─────
 14003
 30041
 ─────
 44044
 ─────
```

2 (a) 11, 22, 33, 44, 55, 66, 77, 88, 99 are palindromic numbers.

(b) One-stage palindromic numbers: 12, 13, 14, 15, 16, 17, 18, 20, 21, 23, 24, 25, 26, 27, 29, 30, 31, 32, 34, 35, 36, 38, 40, 41, 42, 43, 45, 47, 50, 51, 52, 53, 54, 56, 60, 61, 62, 63, 65, 70, 71, 72, 74, 80, 81, 83, 90, 92

(c) Two-stage numbers: 19, 28, 37, 39, 46, 48, 49, 57, 58, 64, 67, 73, 75, 76, 82, 84, 85, 91, 93, 94

(d) Three-stage numbers: 59, 68, 86, 95

(e) Four-stage numbers: 69, 78, 87, 96

(f) Six-stage numbers: 79, 97

To carry out the above investigation is not as big a task as it may seem, for when children find that a number such as 18 is a one-stage palindromic number, it is immediately evident that so also is 81. However many stages a number takes to become palindromic, the number formed by reversing its digits will take the same number of stages.

The numbers 89 and 98, however, are not palindromic even after 20 stages, and children should be warned about this. They can be given calculators to attempt these challenges, although finding which numbers less than 100 are palindromic is an excellent way to practise addition of two-, three- and four-digit numbers. Children will be much more motivated to do these additions than just to work out a lot of sums without an overall purpose.

Shopping at a barter market (page 36)

Children can draw up a table in order to answer the questions.

1 (a) 6 tomatoes
(b) 15 apples
(c) 30 potatoes

2 (a) 5 lettuces
(b) 4 lettuces
(c) 6 lettuces

3 (a) 10 apples
(b) 50 apples
(c) 25 apples
(d) 30 apples

4 (a) 5 lettuces
(b) 10 tomatoes
(c) 50 potatoes

Lettuces	Tomatoes	Apples	Potatoes
1	2	5	10
2	4	10 (3a)	20
3	6 (1a)	15 (1b)	30 (1c)
4 (2b)	8	20	40
5 (2a)	10	25	50
6 (2c)	12	30	60
7	14	35	70
8	16	40	80

5 10 tomatoes = 5 lettuces
10 apples = 2 lettuces
∴ Total trade = 7 lettuces

6 (a) 8 lettuces
(b) 40 apples
(c) 80 potatoes

Using a table is one way to solve these problems. Another method uses ratios or proportion.

For 2(a): since 2 tomatoes are worth 1 lettuce, 10 tomatoes (which is 5 lots of 2) are worth 5 lettuces (5 lots of 1).

For 2(b): since 5 apples are worth 1 lettuce, 20 apples (which is 4 lots of 5) are worth 4 lettuces (which is 4 lots of 1).

Tree diagrams (page 37)

1
```
H H H
H H T
H T H
H T T
T H H
T H T
T T H
T T T
```
Note the systematic way in which the possibilities are written out.

2

Bread	Filling
brown	honey
brown	cheese
brown	Marmite
brown	tuna
brown	salad
white	honey
white	cheese
white	Marmite
white	tuna
white	salad

3 Reading along all the branches, there are nine possibilities:

train/walking	coach/walking	car/walking
train/bus	coach/bus	car/bus
train/taxi	coach/taxi	car/taxi

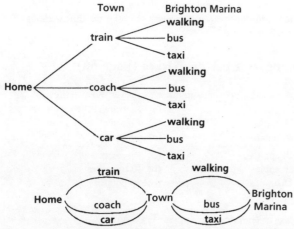

Number patterns (page 38)

1 $37 \times 12 = 444$
$37 \times 15 = 555$

2 (a) $91 \times 5 = 455$ (b) $9109 \times 5 = 45\,545$
$91 \times 6 = 546$ $9109 \times 6 = 54\,654$

3 $143 \times 28 = 4004$
$143 \times 35 = 5005$

4 $131 \times 11\,111 = 1\,455\,541$
$131 \times 111\,111 = 14\,555\,541$

5 $101 \times 22\,222 = 2\,244\,422$
$101 \times 222\,222 = 22\,444\,422$

6 $101 \times 33\,333 = 3\,366\,633$
$101 \times 333\,333 = 336\,666\,633$

7 $37 \times 3333 = 123\,321$
$37 \times 33\,333 = 1\,233\,321$

8 $1234 \times 9 + 5 = 11\,111$
$12\,345 \times 9 + 6 = 111\,111$

9 $9876 \times 9 + 4 = 88\,888$
$98\,765 \times 9 + 3 = 888\,888$

10 $1234 \times 8 + 4 = 9876$
$12\,345 \times 8 + 5 = 98\,765$

11 $11\,111^2 = 123\,454\,321$
$111\,111^2 = 12\,345\,654\,321$

12 $3367 \times 132 = 444\,444$
$3367 \times 165 = 555\,555$

13 $37\,037 \times 12 = 444\,444$
$37\,037 \times 15 = 555\,555$

14 $999\,999 \times 5 = 4\,999\,995$
$999\,999 \times 6 = 5\,999\,994$

Number squares 2 (page 39)

In solving these problems, you can use guess-and-check and/or the given procedure and starting points.

1

2	2	1	5	10	A = 2
5	3	5	4	17	B = 5
3	3	1	4	11	C = 1
5	4	2	1	12	D = 4
15	12	9	14		E = 3

From the first row,
C + B = 6. Now, either use guess-and-check for B and C or use the fact that
C + B = 6 to find the value of D in the fourth row or the fourth column. For the latter method:
$$B + D + A + C = 12$$
$$6 + D + 2 = 12,$$
since A = 2 and B + C = 6
$$\therefore D = 4$$
Since B + C = 6, we can work out C in the third column:
$$\underline{C + B} + C + A = 9$$
$$\quad 6 \quad + C + 2 = 9$$
$$\therefore C = 1$$

2

2	1	2	3	8	A = 1
4	4	1	3	12	B = 3
5	2	4	1	12	C = 4
1	5	3	4	13	D = 2
12	12	10	11		E = 5

Suggested start: A + B = 4

3

3	5	1	2	11	A = 2
3	1	4	2	10	B = 4
5	2	1	3	11	C = 1
1	2	4	5	12	D = 5
12	10	10	12		E = 3

Suggested start: C + D = 6

4

4	4	5	2	15	A = 1
5	5	1	2	13	B = 4
3	1	2	3	9	C = 2
3	2	4	5	14	D = 5
15	12	12	12		E = 3

Suggested start: A + C = 3

Strange maths symbols 2 (page 40)

Children are not expected to use symbols in writing the rules.

1 $\square \odot \triangle = \square + \triangle + 5$
$7 \odot 3 = 7 + 3 + 5$
$= 15$
Rule: Add the two numbers, then add 5.

2 $\square \wedge \triangle = \square - \triangle + 2$
$8 \wedge 2 = 8 - 2 + 2$
$= 8$
Rule: Subtract the second number from the first and add 2.

3 $\square \star \triangle = \square + 2 \times \triangle$
$6 \star 2 = 6 + 2 \times 2$
$= 10$
Rule: Double the second number and add the first to the result.

4 $\square \# \triangle = \dfrac{\square + \triangle}{2}$
$3 \# 1 = \dfrac{3 + 1}{2} = 2$
Rule: Add the two numbers and halve the result.

5 $\square\; \heartsuit\; \triangle = (\square - \triangle)^2$
$6 \heartsuit 1 = 5^2$
$\qquad = 25$
Rule: Subtract the second number from the first and square the result.

6 $\square\; \vee\; \triangle = (\square + \triangle) \times 2$
$2 \vee 4 \;\; = 12$
Rule: Add the two numbers and double the result.

7 $\square\; \oslash\; \triangle = 2 \times \square + \triangle$
$4 \oslash 3 \;\; = 8 + 3$
$\qquad = 11$
Rule: Double the first number and add the second to the result.

8 $\square\; \blacktriangle\; \triangle = \square \div 2 + \triangle$
$10 \blacktriangle 2 = 7$
Rule: Halve the first number and add the second to the result.

9 Making up their own symbols gives children a chance to explore further.

What is my question? (page 41)

Children could be given these exercises without any prior preparation or discussion and the one with the most solutions rewarded. They should discuss their methods with one another. Ideally, the factors should be tested systematically; however, it is likely that some will do it this way.

1 $\begin{array}{c} 60 \\ \underline{2} \\ 120 \end{array} \times \begin{array}{c} 30 \\ \underline{4} \\ 120 \end{array} \times \begin{array}{c} 15 \\ \underline{8} \\ 120 \end{array} \times \begin{array}{c} 40 \\ \underline{3} \\ 120 \end{array} \times \begin{array}{c} 20 \\ \underline{6} \\ 120 \end{array} \times \begin{array}{c} 24 \\ \underline{5} \\ 120 \end{array} \times$

2 $\begin{array}{c} 70 \\ \underline{2} \\ 140 \end{array} \times \begin{array}{c} 35 \\ \underline{4} \\ 140 \end{array} \times \begin{array}{c} 20 \\ \underline{7} \\ 140 \end{array} \times \begin{array}{c} 28 \\ \underline{5} \\ 140 \end{array} \times$

3 $\begin{array}{c} 75 \\ \underline{2} \\ 150 \end{array} \times \begin{array}{c} 50 \\ \underline{3} \\ 150 \end{array} \times \begin{array}{c} 30 \\ \underline{5} \\ 150 \end{array} \times \begin{array}{c} 25 \\ \underline{6} \\ 150 \end{array} \times$

4 $\begin{array}{c} 72 \\ \underline{2} \\ 144 \end{array} \times \begin{array}{c} 36 \\ \underline{4} \\ 144 \end{array} \times \begin{array}{c} 18 \\ \underline{8} \\ 144 \end{array} \times \begin{array}{c} 48 \\ \underline{3} \\ 144 \end{array} \times \begin{array}{c} 24 \\ \underline{6} \\ 144 \end{array} \times \begin{array}{c} 16 \\ \underline{9} \\ 144 \end{array} \times$

5 $\begin{array}{c} 50 \\ \underline{5} \\ 250 \end{array} \times$ **6** $\begin{array}{c} 66 \\ \underline{2} \\ 132 \end{array} \times \begin{array}{c} 33 \\ \underline{4} \\ 132 \end{array} \times \begin{array}{c} 44 \\ \underline{3} \\ 132 \end{array} \times \begin{array}{c} 22 \\ \underline{6} \\ 132 \end{array} \times$

7 $\begin{array}{c} 68 \\ \underline{2} \\ 136 \end{array} \times \begin{array}{c} 34 \\ \underline{4} \\ 136 \end{array} \times \begin{array}{c} 17 \\ \underline{8} \\ 136 \end{array} \times$ **8** $\begin{array}{c} 50 \\ \underline{4} \\ 200 \end{array} \times \begin{array}{c} 25 \\ \underline{8} \\ 200 \end{array} \times \begin{array}{c} 40 \\ \underline{5} \\ 200 \end{array} \times$

Digit puzzles (page 42)

1 (a) 6 possibilities
56 or, with a tree
57 diagram:
65
67
75
76

(b) 9 possibilities
55   75
56   76
57   77
65
66
67

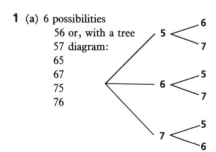

2 (a) 6 possibilities
567 or, with a tree
576 diagram:
657
675
756
765

(b) 27 possibilities
555   655   755
556   656   756
557   657   757
565   665   765
566   666   766
567   667   767
575   675   775
576   676   776
577   677   777

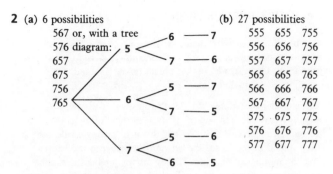

3 The first method given is difficult, and should be explained only to the extremely talented student.

1st digit can be chosen in 4 different ways.
2nd digit can be chosen in 3 different ways.
3rd digit can be chosen in 2 different ways.
4th digit can be chosen in 1 way only.
∴ Total number of possibilities $= 4 \times 3 \times 2 \times 1$
$\qquad\qquad\qquad\qquad\qquad = 24$

or

List the possibilities starting with 5:
5678   5768   5867
5687   5786   5876

If we start with 6, 7 or 8, in each case there are again 6 possibilities, and so there is a total of 24.

or

List all 24 possibilities, working systematically.

or

Use a tree diagram:

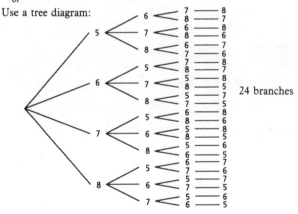

24 branches

4 (a) (i) 2 (for 5 and 15)
    (ii) 11 (for 2, 12, 20, 21, 22, 23, 24, 25, 26, 27)
    (iii) 2 (for 10 and 20)
(b) (i) 19 (for 5, 15, 25, 35, 45, 50, 51, 52, 53, 54, 55, 56, 57, 58, 59, 65, 75, 85)
    (ii) 19 (for 2, 12, 20, 21, 22, 23, 24, 25, 26, 27, 28, 29, 32, 42, 52, 62, 72, 82)
    (iii) 8 (for 10, 20, 30, 40, 50, 60, 70, 80)

Matchstick puzzles (page 43)

Children will need to know their two, three and five times tables to succeed with these exercises. Encourage them to express each rule in words; in the rule formulas, □ stands for the number of original shapes.

1 The number of matches is twice the number of triangles plus 1. Many children will say that the number of matches is going up (or increasing) by 2, but this is not really a rule and they should be led to see the relationship between the figures and the number of matches. If they cannot predict the number for the tenth diagram, they will have to complete the table with figures 6 to 10.

Rule

Triangles	1	2	3	4	5	⟶ 10
Matches	3	5	7	9	11	⟶ 21

2 × □ + 1

2

Squares	1	2	3	4	5	⟶ 10
Matches	4	7	10	13	16	⟶ 31

3 × □ + 1

3

Hexagons	1	2	3	4	5	⟶ 10
Matches	6	11	16	21	26	⟶ 51

5 × □ + 1

4

Houses	1	2	3	4	5	⟶ 10
Matches	6	11	16	21	26	⟶ 51

5 × □ + 1

5

Double squares	1	2	3	4	5	⟶ 10
Matches	7	12	17	22	27	⟶ 52

5 × □ + 2

Problem solving: Your own strategy 1 (page 44)

Children could draw up tables for questions 1, 2 and 3.

1

Day	Number of pages read by Nancy	Number of pages read by Lucy
Monday	9	7
Tuesday	18	14
Wednesday	27	21
Thursday	36	28
Friday	45	35
Saturday	54	42

Therefore Nancy will finish page 54 on Saturday, and on that day Lucy will finish page 42.

2

Day	1	2	3	4	5	6	7
Fine	1p	2p	4p	8p	16p	32p	64p

Therefore Ritu's book is 7 days overdue.

3

Salma	4	8	12	16	20	24	28	32
Becky	3	6	9	12	15	18	21	24

Therefore Salma will fill 32 buckets in this time.

4 Use logical reasoning in this question.

Jim's score = 3 × 7 + 3 × 5
= 36
Michael's score = 37

Michael threw one dart in area A for 7 points, so his score in area B is 30. Therefore Michael threw 6 darts in area B.

5 In 6 days:
the eldest child drinks 3 pints;
the two younger children drink 9 pints
the parents drink 2 pints;
Altogether, the family drinks 14 pints of milk in 6 days.

6 Working backwards is a good strategy. Four 50p coins are worth £2, so her 20p coins are worth £1. Therefore Heidi has five 20p coins.

Since she has one less 20p coin than 10p, she has six 10p coins.

Since she has twice as many 10p coins as 5p, she has three 5p coins.

Her coins are therefore:

5p	10p	20p	50p
3	6	5	4

Problem solving: Your own strategy 2 (page 45)

These solutions show possible strategies. Children should be encouraged to find their own and explain them.

1 Start with the amount Scott has now and work backwards:
Scott has £9.20.
Before he bought the drink, he had £10.00.
Before he was paid for the gardening, he had £2.00.
Before he bought the present he had £4.50, which is the amount of his pocket money.

2 Again work backwards:
We know that Leah weighs 65 kg.
Without Ramah, the scale dropped 38 kg.
Without Andrew, the scale dropped 24 kg.
Therefore Ramah weighs 38 kg and Andrew weighs 24 kg.

3 Note that a total of 39 drinks are served to only 35 people. Therefore, 4 people drink both.

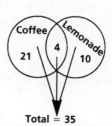

Total = 35

4 Draw up a table and look for a pattern.

Night	Pages read	Page reached
1	11	11
2	9	20
3	7	27
4	5	32
5	3	35
6	1	36

On the sixth night, Shing finished her novel.

5 Working backwards: 5 sweets left plus 12 sweets given away make a total of 17 sweets.

6 Each ice-cream cost 80p. The cost of the chips is unnecessary data.

7 Miss Major sold 30 tickets and has to sell 90 more. The cost of the ticket is unnecessary data.

8 3 apples = 2 oranges or, in a table:
6 apples = 4 oranges
12 apples = 8 oranges

Apples	Oranges
3	2
6	4
9	6
12	8

9 If 2 folders cost £5, I can buy:
    4 for £10
    6 for £15
    8 for £20
    10 for £25

10 6 mugs cost £18.
  (a) Halve both the amount of money and the number of mugs:
    3 mugs cost £9.
  (b) Double both the amount of money and the number of mugs:
    12 mugs cost £36.

Make a model, act it out (page 46)

To solve this puzzle, children could be given – or asked to construct — a board and be provided with counters.

1

2 To solve these problems, it is helpful to use a model. Children should also be provided with 4 × 4 grid paper (p 85).

(a)   **(b)**   **(c)**

Measurement puzzles (page 47)

1 (a) Fill the 7 ℓ bucket. From it, fill the smaller bucket, which will take 3 ℓ 4 ℓ will remain.

(b) Continuing from (a), empty the 3 ℓ bucket.
There are 4 ℓ left in the larger bucket; use this to refill the 3 ℓ bucket; 1 ℓ will remain.

(c) Fill the 3 ℓ bucket and pour the contents into the larger one.
Repeat this. The larger bucket now contains 6 ℓ. Fill the 3 ℓ bucket again and from it fill the larger one, which will take 1 ℓ.
2 ℓ will remain.

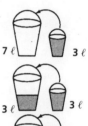

(d) Continuing from (c), first empty the larger bucket, then pour into it the water remaining in the small one (2 ℓ). Refill the 3 ℓ bucket and pour its contents into the larger one, which will then contain 5 ℓ.

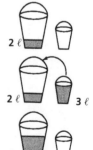

(e) The last stage of (c) has 7 ℓ in one bucket and 2 ℓ in the other, making a total of 9 ℓ.

Children may find other valid solutions.

75

2 Fill the 5 ℓ bucket, and from it fill the smaller one (3 ℓ). It now contains 2 ℓ.

Empty the smaller bucket, and into it pour the 2 ℓ left in the larger one.

Refill the 5 ℓ bucket.

The two together now hold 7 ℓ.

or

Fill the 3 ℓ bucket and pour its contents into the 5 ℓ one.

Again fill the smaller bucket and use it to fill the larger one. It now contains only 1 ℓ.

Now empty the 5 ℓ bucket, and into it pour the 1 ℓ remaining in the smaller one.

Refill the smaller bucket and pour the contents (3 ℓ) into the larger one, which will then contain 4 ℓ.

Again fill the 3 ℓ.

The two together now hold 7 ℓ.

Find my three numbers (page 48)

Logical thinking is needed in answering these questions, and most of them require the children to use guess-and-check strategy as well.

1 △ = 4, ○ = 3, □ = 2
Start with the fact that three △s equal 12, so that △ = 4. Now, △ + ○ = 7, so ○ = 3; and since □ + □ makes 4, □ = 2.
2 □ = 9, △ = 3, ○ = 6
3 △ = 6, ○ = 2, □ = 3
4 ○ = 8, △ = 4, □ = 9

5 □ = 5, △ = 10, ○ = 3
6 △ = 6, ○ = 2, □ = 3
7 △ = 9, □ = 4, ○ = 6
8 ○ = 7, □ = 6, △ = 3
9 □ = 9, ○ = 6, △ = 3
10 △ = 7, ○ = 5, □ = 2

Fraction fun (page 49)

Children should have counters — or some other concrete material — available if they want to work out the problems with the use of some tangible aid.

Children could ask:

1 10	Half of what number is 5?	**6** $\frac{1}{2}$
2 $\frac{1}{2}$	What fraction of 8 is 4?	**7** $\frac{1}{4}$
3 12	One quarter of what number is 3?	**8** $\frac{1}{4}$
4 24	One quarter of what number is 6?	**9** 30
5 $\frac{1}{2}$	What fraction of 18 is 9?	**10** $\frac{1}{10}$

11 $\frac{1}{4}$ **16** $\frac{1}{2}$ **21** $\frac{1}{3}$ **26** $\frac{1}{5}$
12 $\frac{1}{2}$ **17** 27 **22** $\frac{1}{2}$ **27** $\frac{1}{10}$
13 $\frac{1}{5}$ **18** 16 **23** 32 **28** $\frac{1}{6}$
14 40 **19** 20 **24** $\frac{1}{5}$ **29** 30
15 50 **20** 90 **25** $\frac{1}{3}$ **30** 24

Fractions can be used to stimulate able children even though they are becoming less important in primary schools.

Coin puzzles (page 50)

Children can answer these questions either by using guess-and-check or by acting out the problems, as illustrated in 1(a) and (b) and in 2(a).

1 (a) Take 47 counters. Use 7 to begin the first pile. Now divide the remaining 40 equally between the two piles.
(b) Take 34 counters. Use 8 to begin the first pile. Now divide the remaining 26 equally between the two piles.

	1st pile	2nd pile
(a)	27	20
(b)	21	13
(c)	8	15
(d)	36	12
(e)	24	6

2 (a) Take 27 counters. Use 3 to begin the second pile. Now, since the third pile has 3 more than the second, in fact it has 6 more than the first, so place 6 counters in the third pile. Now 18 counters remain, which are divided equally between the three.

	1st pile	2nd pile	3rd pile
(a)	6	9	12
(b)	20	11	10
(c)	8	16	32
(d)	6	12	3
(e)	3	6	12
(f)	21	10	7

Problems on a dartboard (page 51)

1 (a) 3, 5, 6, 8, 9, 10, 11, 12 and all further numbers are possible.

(b) 1, 2, 4 and 7 are the only impossible scores. Most children will use trial and error. Once three consecutive possible scores are found — 8, 9 and 10 — there is no need to search further; you can add 3 to any of these, so that all remaining numbers are possible.

3 + 3 =	6
3 + 5 =	8
3 + 3 + 3 =	9
5 + 5 =	10
3 + 3 + 5 =	11
3 + 3 + 3 + 3 =	12
3 + 5 + 5 =	13
3 + 3 + 3 + 5 =	14
5 + 5 + 5 =	15

2 (a) 2, 4, 6, 7, 8, 9 and all further numbers are possible.

(b) 1, 3 and 5 are the only impossible scores. This time, once we have two consecutive possible scores the search is over.

2 + 2 =	4
2 + 2 + 2 =	6
7 =	7
2 + 2 + 2 + 2 =	8
2 + 7 =	9

3 Since the scores are all odd numbers and since four odd numbers give an even number, none of the odd numbers is a possible total.

9 + 7 + 3 + 3 =	22
9 + 9 + 3 + 1 =	22
7 + 7 + 3 + 1 =	18
9 + 9 + 3 + 3 =	24
7 + 3 + 3 + 3 =	16

4 List all possible combinations that would achieve a score of 34.

(a) Smallest number of throws is 6.

(b) Greatest number of throws is 17.

9	6	2	No. of throws
0	0	17	17
0	1	14	15
0	2	11	13
0	3	8	11
2	0	8	10
0	4	5	9
2	2	2	6

Goldbach's conjectures (page 52)

Only some of the possible answers are listed for each exercise.

1 (a) 3 + 13, 5 + 11

(b) 5 + 19, 7 + 17, 11 + 13

(c) 3 + 43, 5 + 41, 17 + 29, 23 + 23

(d) 5 + 79, 11 + 73, 13 + 71, 17 + 67, 23 + 61, 31 + 53, 37 + 47, 41 + 43

(e) 3 + 89, 13 + 79, 19 + 73, 31 + 61

(f) 5 + 67, 11 + 61, 13 + 59, 19 + 53, 29 + 43, 31 + 41

(g) 7 + 31, 19 + 19

(h) 19 + 79, 31 + 67, 37 + 61

2 (a) 9 = 2 + 2 + 5 = 3 + 3 + 3

(b) 23 = 5 + 7 + 11 = 5 + 5 + 13

(c) 29 = 5 + 11 + 13 = 7 + 11 + 11 = 3 + 13 + 13

(d) 33 = 3 + 13 + 17 = 5 + 11 + 17 = 7 + 7 + 19 = 3 + 11 + 19

(e) 35 = 5 + 11 + 19 = 7 + 11 + 17 = 3 + 13 + 19

(f) 53 = 23 + 11 + 19 = 7 + 23 + 23 = 17 + 17 + 19

(g) 83 = 61 + 19 + 3 = 61 + 11 + 11 = 5 + 19 + 59

(h) 69 = 53 + 13 + 3 = 53 + 11 + 5 = 3 + 7 + 59

Domino puzzles (page 53)

Children should be provided with grid paper in empty domino shapes (see p. 88), and should also be given dominoes to work with. They need to act out these problems.

Only one solution is shown for exercises 1(b)–1(e) and exercise 2. There are several other answers when the squares are rotated.

1 (a)

(b) (c) (d) (e)

2 This exercise is quite difficult, as children will have to work out what the sum of each side is to be as well as how to place the dominoes.

(a) (b) (c)

(d) (e)

Boat trips (page 54)

It is advisable for children to act out this problem, using models. It would be very difficult to conceptualise without either doing this or drawing a model (as illustrated for a group of eight people).

Waiting to cross	Crossing or returning	After crossing
8	0	0
5	3 →	0
5	1 ←	2
3	3 →	2
3	1 ←	4
1	3 →	4
1	1 ←	6
0	2 →	6
0	0	8

1 Note the pattern that emerges.

Number of people	Number of trips
1	1
→ 2	1
3	1
→ 4	3
5	3
→ 6	5
7	5
→ 8	7
9	7
→ 10	9
11	9
→ 12	11

2

	People	Trips
(a)	20	19
	21	19
(b)	22	21

3 The pattern for the number of trips is very interesting, as it consists of each odd number repeated. However, when we are looking for patterns we always want to see if we can establish a relationship between the numbers in the first column and the numbers in the second column.

In this case, if the number of people wishing to cross the river is even, the number of trips required is one less than the number of people.

If the number of people is odd, then the number of trips is two less than the number of people.

Cake-cutting time (page 55)

This experiment can be done in class using pikelets, or modelling clay rolled out flat and cut into circles with an upturned cup or glass.

Alternatively, provide children with copies of sheets on which blank circles have been drawn.

1 2 diameters: all angles at centre are 90°

2 Some possible solutions

3

4 3 diameters: all angles at centre are 60°

5   **6**

7 4 diameters: all angles at centre are 45°

8 First cut in half , then place one half on top of the other or (if using models) first cut horizontally; then, with pieces stacked, cut as shown

The locker problem (page 56)

Lockers numbered 1, 4, 9, 16 and 25 are open. These locker numbers correspond to square numbers.

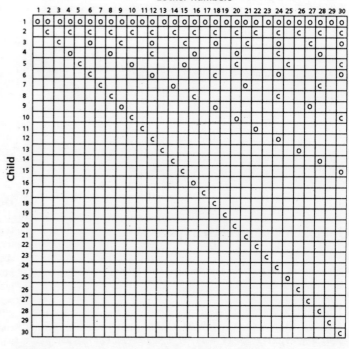

Locker numbers

Find the correct position (page 57)

1

2 Children can either construct the cube by making and cutting out a net of a cube (illustrated at right) or use logic to answer the questions.

(a) From the first and second views, the shapes on the faces adjacent (next) to ☐ are ★, ◐, △ and ⊙, so the sixth shape is ●
   Therefore, ● is opposite ☐.

(b) Similarly, from the second, third and fourth views, the shapes adjacent to ⊙ are △, ●, ☐ and ◑. Therefore, the sixth shape, ★, is opposite ⊙.

(c) △

Problem solving: Using tables 2 (page 58)

1

Michelle's contribution	Mia's contribution	Total cost
£16	£8	£24

2

Imran	Gordon	Bruce	Sum of their ages
16	11	8	35

It will be easier if you first guess Bruce's age and then work out the ages of the others.

3

Monique	Laura	Amy	Sum of their ages
12	8	5	25

4

Lemon drops (20p a pkt)	Chocolate mints (5p each)	Total spent
4 packages (12 sweets)	8	£1.20

5

	Raspberries at £3	Grapes at £4	Cost
(a)	2 kg	3 kg	£18
(b)	4 kg	0	£12
	0	3 kg	£12
	2 kg	1½ kg	
	3 kg	¾ kg	
	1 kg	2¼ kg	£12
	1⅓ kg	2 kg	
	2⅔ kg	1 kg	

There are many possible answers to 5(b) and only some are given here *in the table*. Children are unlikely to give more than the first two.

All the solutions can be represented on the graph; some are indicated by the dots:

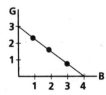

An informal discussion about all the possible solutions is worthwhile.

The four 5's challenge (page 59)

Children must take special care with the order of operations. It would be a good idea to let them check one another's work before showing it to the teacher.

These are some possible solutions. There are many others.

Note: $\sqrt[5]{5^5} \div 5$ (see exercise 2) might seem a very difficult solution to come from such young mathematicians, but in fact it was an answer given to the author by a 10-year-old. ($\sqrt[5]{5^5}$ = the fifth root of 5 to the power of 5. Since $\sqrt{5^2} = 5$, the child concluded the above.)

1 $5 + 5 - 5 - 5 = 0$
  $(5 - 5) \times (5 - 5) = 0$
  $(5 + 5) \times (5 - 5) = 0$
  $(5 \times 5) \times (5 - 5) = 0$
  $5 \times (5 - 5) \div 5 = 0$

2 $(5 \div 5) \times (5 \div 5) = 1$
  $\sqrt[5]{5^5} \div 5 = 1$

3 $5 \div 5 + 5 \div 5 = 2$
  $(\sqrt{5 \times 5} + 5) \div 5 = 2$

4 $(5 + 5 + 5) \div 5 = 3$

5 $(5 \times 5 - 5) \div 5 = 4$
  $\sqrt{5 \times 5} - (5 \div 5) = 4$

6 $\sqrt{5 \times 5} + 5 - 5 = 5$
  $5 \times 5 \div \sqrt{5 \times 5} = 5$
  $\sqrt{5 \times 5} \div .5 - 5 = 5$

7 $\sqrt{5 \times 5} + 5 \div 5 = 6$
  $(5 \times 5 + 5) \div 5 = 6$
  $55 \div 5 - 5 = 6$

8 $\sqrt{5 \times 5} + \sqrt{5 \times 5} = 10$
  $(5 + 5) \times 5 \div 5 = 10$
  $(55 - 5) \div 5 = 10$
  $5 \div .5 + 5 - 5 = 10$

9 $\sqrt{5 \times 5} + 5 + 5 = 15$
  $5 \times 5 - (5 + 5) = 15$
  $5 \times 5 - 5 - 5 = 15$
  $\sqrt{5 \times 5} \div .5 + 5 = 15$
  $5 \div .5 + \sqrt{5} \times \sqrt{5} = 15$

10 $5 \times 5 - (5 \div 5) = 24$

11 $5 \times 5 \times (5 \div 5) = 25$
  $5 \times 5 + 5 - 5 = 25$
  $\sqrt{5 \times 5} \times \sqrt{5 \times 5} = 25$

12 $5 \times 5 + 5 \div 5 = 26$

13 $5 \times 5 + \sqrt{5 \times 5} = 30$
  $5 + 5 \times \sqrt{5 \times 5} = 30$

14 $(5 + 5) \times 5 - 5 = 45$
  $5 \times 5 \times .5 - 5 = 45$

15 $5 \times 5 + 5 \times 5 = 50$
  $55 - \sqrt{5 \times 5} = 50$
  $5! \times .5 - 5 - 5 = 50$

16 $(5 + 5) \times 5 + 5 = 55$
  $55 + 5 - 5 = 55$
  $55 \times 5 \div 5 = 55$
  $5 \times 5 \div .5 + 5 = 55$
  $5! \times .5 - \sqrt{5 \times 5} = 55$

17 $(5 + 5 + 5) \times 5 = 75$

18 $(5 \times 5 - 5) \times 5 = 100$
  $5! + 5 - (5 \times 5) = 100$

19 $5 \times 5 \times 5 - 5 = 120$
  $\sqrt{5 \times 5} - 5 + 5! = 120$

20 $5! + 5 + 5 - 5 = 125$
  $5 \times 5 \times \sqrt{5 \times 5} = 125$
  $5^5 \div 5 \div 5 = 125$

21 $5 \times 5 \times 5 + 5 = 130$
  $5! + 5 + \sqrt{5 \times 5} = 130$

22 $(5 \times 5 + 5) \times 5 = 150$
  $5! + 5 \times 5 + 5 = 150$

Stars and shapes (page 60)

Children should be provided with dot-squared paper (p. 90) for exercise 2 and squared paper (p. 89) for exercise 3.

1 (a) (b) (c)

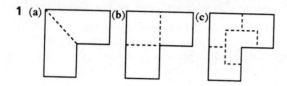

2 (a)

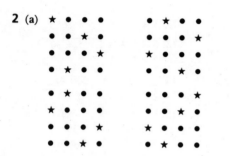

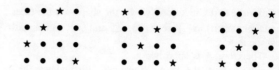

(b)

3

★	★	★	★
		★	★
★		★	
	★	★	

Part 4
Grid paper and diagram masters

The solutions to certain challenges in this book require the use of special grid paper, diagrams or figures. The samples of these in the following pages are photocopiable for classroom use only.

6 mm square paper

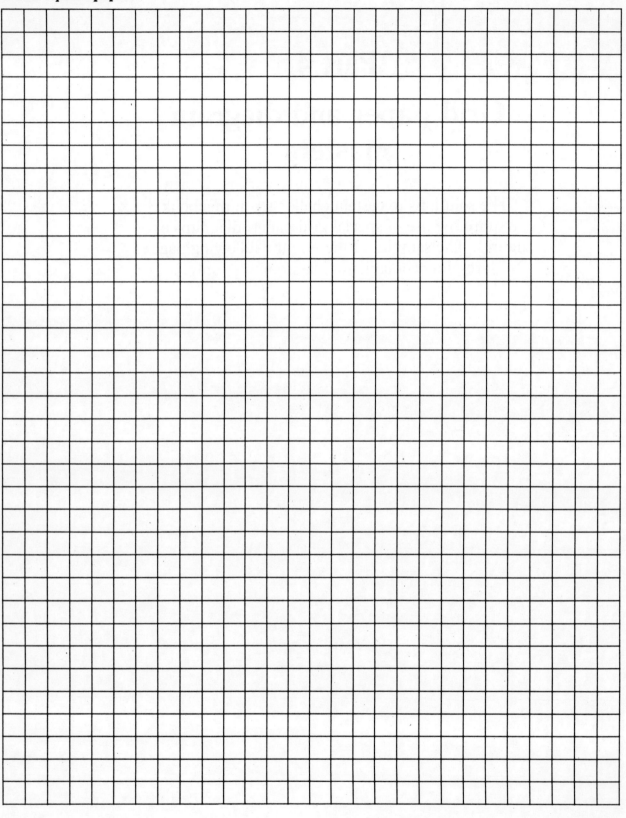

1 cm square paper

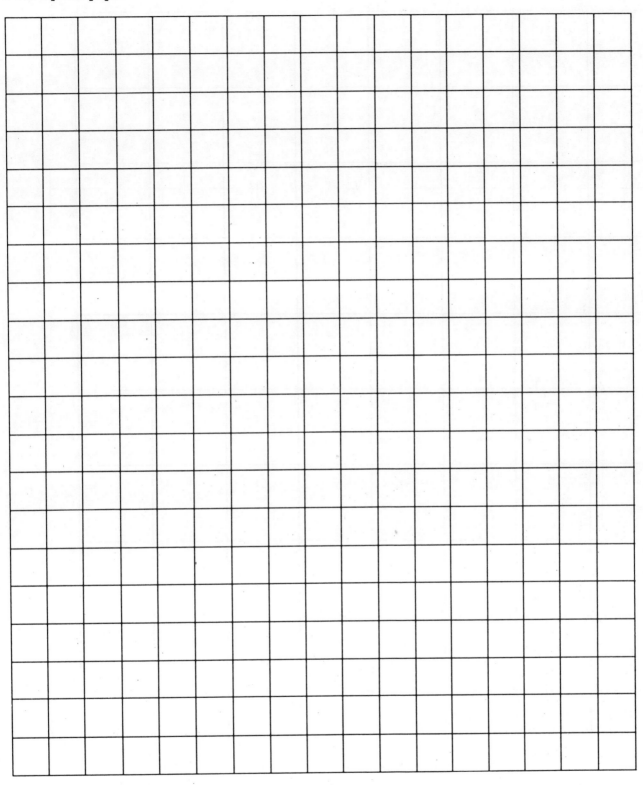

2 cm square paper

© Mathematics Enrichment Book C Simon & Schuster Education 1993

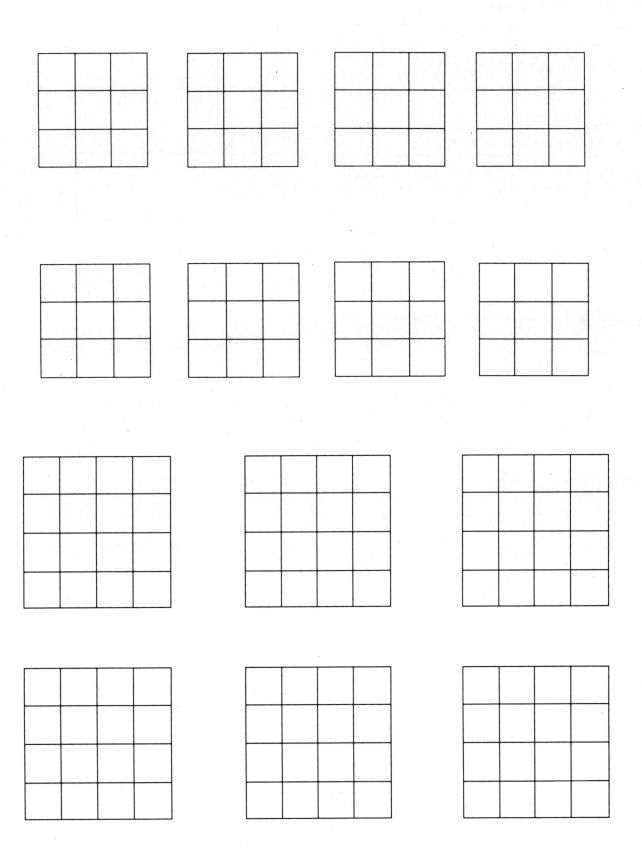

1 cm triangular grid paper

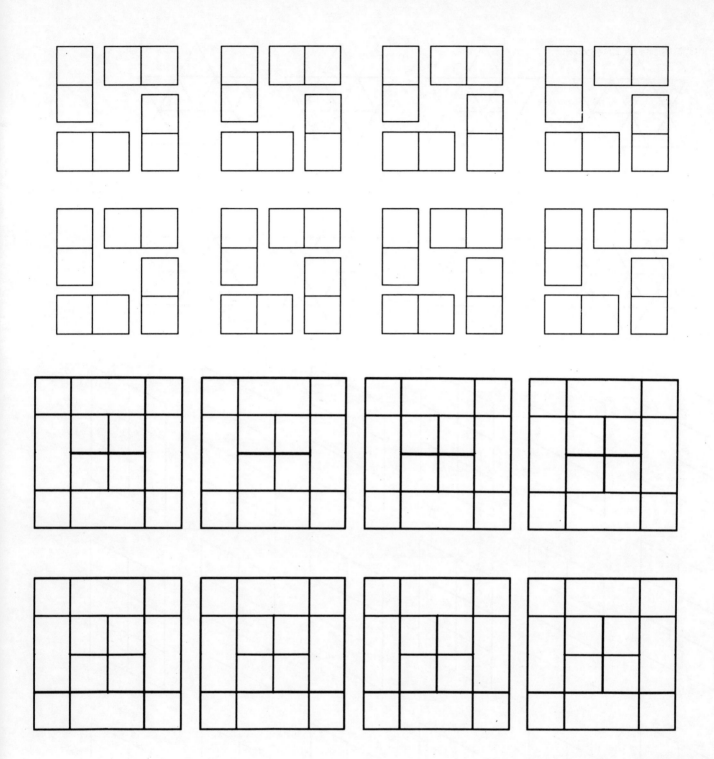

8 mm square dot paper

1 cm square dot paper